Better Living
Through
TELEVISION

The

quote unquote

Guide to Life

Foreword by Matt Roush

BARNES & NOBLE

NEW YORK

Check out the TV Guide® Don't Quote Me®
game for more fun with television quotes!

Special thanks to Steve Scebelo, Karina Reeves, Matt Roush, Ian Birch,
and Nicole Nash at TV Guide. Additional text by Lindsay Herman.

2006 by TV Guide Magazine Group, Inc.

TV Guide® and TV Guide & Design® are registered trademarks of
TV Guide Magazine Group, Inc. and are used with permission.

2006 Barnes & Noble

ISBN-13: 978-0-7607-8233-0
ISBN-10: 0-7607-8233-4

Printed and bound in China

1 3 5 7 9 10 8 6 4 2

•• Contents ••

foreword

Once heard, never forgotten. That's how TV, at its best, works on you. For example, every time I'm feeling even a twinge of self-pity, three simple words from TV act like a dash of water (or a cosmic pie) to the face: *"Oh, poor you!"*

This vicious taunt, from the immortal Livia Soprano to her beleaguered son Tony, both terrifies and amuses me. It's a wake-up call that makes me cringe and laugh each time I recall it, haunting me in the same way Livia forever haunts Tony.

Some have said a picture is worth a thousand words. On TV, which is truly a writer's medium, it's often the opposite: the words provide the picture. We quote from our favorite TV shows for simple reasons. TV is our constant companion, always has been. It's there to comfort and cheer us when we're blue, and reaffirm us when we're happy. Over time, the characters we love best begin to feel like family. And they often say things we didn't know we always wanted to say. (Take Murphy Brown, who memorably growled: "I've experienced life, and I'm here to tell you it's overrated!")

A punchline can carry unexpected symbolic weight. For example, this koan from the Tao of *Friends'* Chandler Bing: "You have to stop the Q-Tip when there's resistance!" Or consider this message of tolerance from the least likely of country bumpkins, *King of the Hill'*s adorably naïve Luanne Platter: "At the beauty academy they teach us that people aren't black or white or yellow or red, but their hair can be." (Talk about taking us back to our roots.) These are words to live by, and that's what this book of TV quotes is all about.

You could build entire philosophy or sociology courses around the life lessons we glean from these eloquent pop-culture icons. They can range from the whimsical musings of *Sex and the City*'s Carrie Bradshaw to the impassioned rants of *Designing Women*'s Julia Sugarbaker and the cynical asides of *Law & Order*'s seen-it-all detective Lennie Briscoe, who once described love as "a dangerous disease instantly cured by marriage."

One of the all-time great TV sages was *Northern Exposure*'s DJ for all seasons, Chris Stevens, who borrowed from music, literature, and movies to create soulful soliloquys that opened the minds of everyone in Cicely, Alaska—and, by extension, the millions who savored this unique series—to the possibilities of life: "As brother Nietzsche said, being human is a complicated gig. So give that ol' dark night of the soul a hug. Howl the eternal yes!" Who could say no?

In these pages, you'll find "Life Lessons" that will help guide you in your quest for better living through television, quizzes that will test your dedication to your TV education, and plenty of quotes filled with wit, and even some wisdom, to help put your own life in perspective.

I know this blustery speech from *Seinfeld*'s Frank Costanza (from the episode where Elaine pilfered from his magazine collection) really resonates with me: "How do you just walk into a house and take a *TV Guide*? How does she expect you to watch TV? Am I just supposed to turn it on and wander aimlessly around the dial?" Truer words were never spoken.

Happy viewing, and reading!

Matt Roush
Senior Critic, *TV Guide*

CHAPTER 1

The Wonder Years

and Other Steps on the Road to Adulthood

The lessons learned during childhood can last a lifetime. On television, children are there to take the pressure off the adults around them by being cute, funny, and even poignant. Like any good TV character, you should remember these aspects of your childhood and use them for comedic or dramatic fodder. If you're having trouble coping, take a tip from Kevin Arnold and try narrating your troubles away. Vocalizing each misstep, accomplishment, and important moment can help put things into perspective (and makes for a great TV show).

"One day you're in DIAPERS; the next day you're gone. But the memories of childhood stay with you for the long haul."

Daniel Stern as narrator Kevin Arnold on *The Wonder Years*

"The FUTURE keeps telling us what the PAST was about. You make the past mean different things by the way you use THE TIME THAT COMES AFTER."

James McDaniel as Lt. Arthur Fancy on *NYPD Blue*

"My mother always used to say: 'The older you get, the better you get, UNLESS YOU'RE A BANANA.'"

Betty White as Rose Nylund on *The Golden Girls*

"When I grow up, I want to be a PRINCIPAL or a CATERPILLAR."

Nancy Cartwright as the voice of Ralph Wiggum on *The Simpsons*

"I learned a secret in school: LMNOP isn't one letter, it's like, seven or ten!"

Stephanie Weir as Dot on *Mad TV*

"Tutors are expensive, y'all just gonna have to WORK HARDER. We can barely afford kids, we can't afford STUPID KIDS."

Terry Crews as Julius on *Everybody Hates Chris*

"If there's anything I can't stand, it's a PERFECT KID. And six of 'em, yecch!"

Ann B. Davis as Alice Nelson on *The Brady Bunch*

Quiz: All About *The Wonder Years*

Nothing quite represents growing up like *The Wonder Years*, the coming-of-age dramedy that featured lovable Kevin Arnold. As adult Kevin reflects on (and narrates) the thoughts and trials of the young Kevin, so must we look back to our own wonder years to better understand our present. How much do you remember about *The Wonder Years*?

1. What neighborhood sweetheart does Kevin spend most of his adolescence pining after?

2. What is bullying brother Wayne's potty-mouthed nickname for Kevin?
   a. turd blossom   c. butthead
   b. pissy pants   d. weenie

3. Paul Pfeiffer, Kevin's geeky foil and lifelong friend, sneezes his way through junior high as a result of hilariously unshakable allergic reactions. What was poor Paul allergic to?

4. True or false: Kevin and company's mind-numbingly monotone science teacher was played by a deadpan Bill Murray.

5. Who wrote the classic song used in *The Wonder Years'* opening credits?

Answers: 1. Winnie Cooper 2. c 3. everything 4. false (it was Ben Stein) 5. John Lennon and Paul McCartney

"Okay, first rule of this carpool. No breaking wind in my car. The only gas that BERNIE MAC wants to be smelling is unleaded."

Bernie Mac on *The Bernie Mac Show*

"Our children are our greatest treasure. They deserve a school board president who doesn't leave her feminine ointments in the fridge next to the mustard. That was the WORST SANDWICH I ever ate!"

Seth McFarlane as the voice of Peter Griffin on *Family Guy*

"As long as you're a TAX DEDUCTION, you'll always be safe in my house."

George Lopez as George on *The George Lopez Show*

"Who's FICA? Why is he getting all my money?"

Jennifer Aniston as Rachel Green on *Friends*

"I'm majoring in economics. Actually, I'm majoring in MONEY, anything to do with MONEY. I've been attached to MONEY ever since I was a kid."

Michael J. Fox as Alex P. Keaton on *Family Ties*

"The next time you put OUTKAST before JESUS I'm gonna cast you out of this house."

Mo'Nique as Nikki Parker on *The Parkers*

"I know STEALING A FOOT is weird. But, hello, living in a house where a foot is AVAILABLE to be stolen is weird."

Lauren Ambrose as Claire Fisher on *Six Feet Under*

"Thank God I did not grow up with a mother who wore a leopard-skin headband, white see-through T-shirt, and glued RHINESTONES to her fingernails."

Dixie Carter as Julia Sugarbaker on *Designing Women*

"You guys are a bunch of cynics, you know that? I mean, what kind of high school memories will you have if all you did in high school was BITCH AND MOAN about everything?"

Meredith Monroe as Andie McPhee on *Dawson's Creek*

"When I was a teenager I wanted to write the Great American Novel. But then I realized that I didn't even want to read the Great American Novel."

Ray Romano as Ray Barone on *Everybody Loves Raymond*

"You want me to drive the LOSER CRUISER?"

Kaley Cuoco as Bridget Hennessay (about a minivan) on *8 Simple Rules*

• Life Lesson •

Don't Be Afraid
of Those Wavy Lines in Your Head....

As Freud knew, one of the secrets to a happy and healthy adult-hood is dealing with the difficult issues you faced as a child. So if you're feeling confused about why you are the way you are, a flash-back might just resolve some of your questions. Tony Soprano, Nate Fisher, and Dylan McKay are just a few of the TV characters who have found peace after reliving some childhood moments; on *Everybody Loves Raymond*, Ray finds out that the root of some of his problems may stem from his parents separating for a year when he was a small child (because of an argument about salt). Be aware, though, that flashing back can sometimes be traumatic—for instance, when Sawyer recalled his parents' deaths on *Lost*, or during the surprisingly common sister-abducted-by-unknown-forces flashback, as seen in such supernatural dramas as *Charmed* and *The X-Files*. Handled properly—and possibly by a professional—however, you may not only understand yourself a little better after a few vivid sessions spent recalling your youth, you just might feel more confident about having sent out headshots of your unsuspecting offspring to the local talent agency.

"I've learned something: SELLING OUT is sweet because when you sell out, you get to make a lot of money, and when you have money, you don't have to hang out with a bunch of poor asses like you guys."

Trey Parker as the voice of Eric Cartman on *South Park*

"I'm not sure if the next part of the show is UNSUITABLE for children at home, but we can only hope."

Drew Carey on *Whose Line Is It Anyway?*

"I may not have had a child, Fleischman, but I KNOW ONE when I SEE ONE."

Janine Turner as Maggie O'Connell on *Northern Exposure*

"Life sure was a lot EASIER when I didn't like boys."

Melissa Gilbert as Laura Ingalls on *Little House on the Prairie*

"I have breasts for the first time and the ONLY MAN in my life doesn't know what to do with them!"

Candice Bergen as Murphy Brown (attempting to breast-feed her newborn son) on *Murphy Brown*

"Nobody knows what kind of parent they'd make until it's TOO LATE to back out."

Miguel Ferrer as Dr. Garrett Macy on *Crossing Jordan*

"I'm glad Trishelle isn't PREGNANT. I'm not ready to be a parent."

Steven Hill on *The Real World: Las Vegas*

"I remember how hard it was when I realized my father was a son of a bitch. I can't imagine what it must be like when you realize you RAISED one."

Sam Waterson as Jack McCoy on *Law & Order*

"Here I am at 5 O'CLOCK IN THE MORNING stuffing bread crumbs up a dead bird's butt."

Roseanne Barr as Roseanne Conner on *Roseanne*

"I discovered a whole new affliction for old age, worse than balding: invisible to TEENAGE GIRLS!"

Timothy Busfield as Elliot Weston on *thirtysomething*

Quiz: TV's Multiples

There's nothing like growing up a twin! Not only do you have a lifelong companion, but having a twin gives you a glimpse at your own life from the outside. Answer true or false to the following questions about TV's most famous multiples.

1. On *The Cosby Show*, Sondra Huxtable Tibideaux gives birth to a set of twins, Nelson and Winnie, both of whom were played by twins.

2. Preston and Porter Scavo are the misbehaving twin brothers on one of television's best primetime soap operas, *Knots Landing*.

3. On *Full House*, Tanner tenant Joey Gladstone and his wife, Rebecca Donaldson, were blessed with twin boys during the show's later years.

4. The *Beverly Hillbillies'* Jethro Bodine and his twin sister, Jethrine, bear an uncanny resemblance because they were played by the same actor.

5. On *Family Affair,* twins Betty and Jenny (along with sister Cissy) are sent to live with their Uncle Bill after the death of their parents.

6. On *The Simpsons*, Marge's sisters are blue-haired, chain-smoking, MacGyver-loving twins who work together at the Department of Motor Vehicles.

7. On twin classic *Sister, Sister*, Tamara is bookish and demure, while Tia is outgoing, flirty, and popular.

Answers: 1. true 2. false 3. false 4. true 5. true 6. false 7. false

"What are we going to do? Sit around bars, SIPPING COSMOS and SLEEPING WITH STRANGERS when we're eighty?"

Sarah Jessica Parker as Carrie Bradshaw on *Sex and the City*

"I'm an ADULT, and I deserve an adult beverage."

Dave Willis as the voice of Meatwad on *Aqua Teen Hunger Force*

"When you two were kids, you used to run around naked and lay in bed with us all night. We bathed you and we cleaned your butts when you pooped, and WE LOVED IT. Now, we try to pat you on the head and you run for the hills. Well, I'm fed up. We are going to be CLOSE from now on whether you like it or not. We're going to spend QUALITY TIME together—and we're going to ENJOY it, damn it!

Joe Flaherty as Harold Weir on *Freaks and Geeks*

"It is said that a man's life can be measured by the DREAMS he fulfills."

Ricardo Montalban as Mr. Roarke on *Fantasy Island*

"We're adults. When did that happen? And how do we make it stop?"

Ellen Pompeo as Dr. Meredith Grey on *Grey's Anatomy*

"BEAUTY FADES. DUMB IS FOREVER."

Judge Judy Sheindlin on *Judge Judy*

CHAPTER 2

Being Yourself

(or a Character of the Same Name)

Although it's often tempting to go hide behind that invisible fourth wall, it's important to remember that you are the main character in the dramedy that is your life. The time-tested formula of actors playing themselves (from Dick Van Dyke to Roseanne) can work well in your life, too! Whether you're a nerd with your pants hiked up to your arm-pits or a man-chasing meddler, be yourself and your "audience" will love you. And if you're really lucky, you'll even get your own spin-off.

"I'm not exactly the PHYSICAL TYPE. I get nosebleeds watching tennis."

Paul Benedict as Harry Bentley on *The Jeffersons*

"I don't DRINK, I don't SMOKE, and I don't DO WINDOWS."

Flip Wilson as Geraldine on *The Flip Wilson Show*

"You know what? You've got SPUNK. I hate spunk."

Ed Asner as Lou Grant on *The Mary Tyler Moore Show*

"I like school...it's a good way to KILL TIME between weekends."

Mark-Paul Gosselaar as Zack Morris on *Saved by the Bell*

"It's hard to be NATURAL when you're wearing a toupee, contact lenses, and four-inch heels."

Jack Riley as Elliot Carlin on *The Bob Newhart Show*

"COP FEET weren't meant for HOOKER SHOES."

Tyne Daley as Mary Beth Lacey on *Cagney & Lacey*

"I have TWO DIFFERENT FEET, why shouldn't I wear two different shoes?"

Soleil Moon Frye as Punky Brewster on *Punky Brewster*

"My name is Todd Foley. I'm a motivational speaker, I am thrice divorced, and I live in a VAN DOWN BY THE RIVER!"

Chris Farley as Todd Foley on *Saturday Night Live*

"I'm Dave Chappelle, and I like Internet porn."

Dave Chappelle on *Chappelle's Show*

"Don't talk to me about Christmas, will ya? All that sticky, phony GOODWILL. I'd like to get a giant candy cane and beat the wings off a sugar-plum fairy."

Jack Klugman as Oscar Madison on *The Odd Couple*

"What a picture of DOMESTIC TRANQUILITY: hemlock on the hearth and my wife feeding the piranha."

John Astin as Gomez Addams on *The Addams Family*

"If my LIFE were like a MOVIE, I'd fall asleep or I'd walk out."

Rachel Griffiths as Brenda Chenowith on *Six Feet Under*

Quiz: Spin-offs

There's no better opportunity to be yourself than when you get your own spin-off. Match the show on the left with the show it was spun off from on the right, and take a lesson from these newly appointed "main characters": the show is all yours.

1. *Rhoda*
2. *The Facts of Life*
3. *Laverne & Shirley*
4. *Different World*
5. *Family Matters*
6. *The Simpsons*
7. *Frasier*
8. *The Jeffersons*
9. *Mork & Mindy*
10. *Strange Love*
11. *Empty Nest*
12. *Just the Ten of Us*
13. *Daria*
14. *Angel*
15. *Maude*

a. *All in the Family*
b. *The Tracey Ullman Show*
c. *The Cosby Show*
d. *Cheers*
e. *The Golden Girls*
f. *Happy Days*
g. *The Mary Tyler Moore Show*
h. *Growing Pains*
i. *Beavis and Butt-head*
j. *Buffy the Vampire Slayer*
k. *Perfect Strangers*
l. *Diff'rent Strokes*
m. *The Surreal Life*

Answers: 1. g, 2. l, 3. f, 4. c, 5. k, 6. b, 7. d, 8. a, 9. f, 10. m, 11. e, 12. h, 13. i, 14. j, 15. a

"I just had another one of my BRILLIANT ideas."

Lisa Whelchel as Blair Warner on *The Facts of Life*

"It's a LITTLE KNOWN FACT that the tan became popular in what is known as the Bronze Age."

John Ratzenberger as Cliff Clavin on *Cheers*

"Mekka LEKKA hi, mekka HINEY ho."

John Paragon as Jambi on *Pee-Wee's Playhouse*

"Sometimes, when I'm really nervous, I stick my hands in my ARMPITS, and I smell them."

Molly Shannon as Mary Katherine Gallagher on *Saturday Night Live*

"The fact that my kid is more concerned with the punishment than the crime tells me something. And you know what it tells me? My kid is a WEENIE."

Catherine Hicks as Annie Camden on *7th Heaven*

"My Homer is not a COMMUNIST. He may be a liar, a pig, an idiot, a communist, but he is not a porn star."

Dan Castellaneta as the voice of Abraham "Grandpa" Simpson on *The Simpsons*

"Did something happen? Was I in the room when it happened?"

William Shatner as Denny Crane on *Boston Legal*

"The first impression I get when I walk into this house is LIBERACE WITH DIARRHEA, 1940."

Charo on *The Surreal Life*

"Yes, yes I am. MASTER of my domain."

Jerry Seinfeld on *Seinfeld*

"When Wade and I were first married, he begged me to be practical, but thank God I lived by my credo: 'Veni, vidi, visa—I came, I saw, I CHARGED IT.'"

Swoosie Kurtz as Alexandra Reed Halsey Barker on *Sisters*

"Just 'cause I said 'yes' when we got married don't mean I gotta KEEP SAYIN' 'yes' all the rest of my life."

Jean Stapleton as Edith Bunker on *All in the Family*

"When you married me you knew that I couldn't cook, I couldn't sew, and I couldn't keep house. All I could do was talk Hungarian and do imitations of ZSA ZSA GABOR."

Eva Gabor as Lisa Douglas on *Green Acres*

• Life Lesson •

Your Personal Reality (TV Show)

There's no better time to be yourself than in front of a nationwide TV audience. So why not apply to become a contestant or house member on your favorite reality show? The key is to pick the show that best matches your true self. If you've got an MBA in your pocket and don't mind offensive hairpieces, *The Apprentice* may be your program of choice. If you're on the prowl for love, dating shows like *Blind Date, Date My Mom*, and the *Bachelor* or *Bachelorette* are excellent ways to meet your potential match. And if you possess a unique skill, you could be generating some serious cash flow on one of the many talent-oriented programs—such as *The Chef, America's Next Top Model* (if you're upwards of five-foot-nine, natch), or *American Idol*. Once you arrive on your reality show of choice, be sure to be yourself to the fullest, and leave your mark with as much chutzpah as possible—let loose those claws and prescription drug addictions! Because if you are a truly memorable cast member, you may get an opportunity to bask in that sixteenth minute of spotlight when the producers of the *Surreal Life* come knocking.

"There's a time to be DANIEL BOONE, and there's a time to be a plumber."

Richard Dean Anderson as Angus MacGyver on *MacGyver*

"Even Hemingway wasn't good at being Hemingway."

Peter Horton as Prof. Gary Shepherd on *thirtysomething*

"In my dream, I'm on the subway completely naked. And then, all of a sudden, that HOT GARDENER from *Desperate Housewives* gets on, and he puts his hand on my breast. Then that HOT SMART GUY from *Jeopardy!* gets on and puts his hand on my other breast. Then that HOT KOREAN GUY from *Lost* gets on and puts his hand on my other breast. Oh, yeah, in this dream I have three breasts."

Debra Messing as Grace Adler on *Will & Grace*

"I want him to see someone on the street who's BEAUTIFUL and say, 'You know what? She might wear a retainer to bed,' or, 'You know what? Like, that girl might just have pooped her pants.'"

Erika Rumsey on *Beauty and the Geek*

"I'm planning to take a crap later. Would you like to be kept informed about that?"

Dennis Franz as Det. Andy Sipowicz on *NYPD Blue*

"I fail to comprehend your indignation, sir. I have simply made the LOGICAL DEDUCTION that you are a LIAR."

Leonard Nimoy as Mr. Spock on *Star Trek*

"Did I BREATHE and give you the impression that I was done speaking?"

Judge Marilyn Milian on *The People's Court*

"I CRINGE whenever you empty your pockets—
you put your change in neat little piles. And
I'm not too crazy that you hang your underwear
on hangers."

Jack Klugman as Oscar Madison on *The Odd Couple*

"Clark's sense of humor is an acquired taste; much
like his sense of fashion."

Erica Durance as Lois Lane on *Smallville*

"It took all day, but I finally found the PERFECT
PAIR of alligator pumps to wear to the Save the
Everglades dinner tonight."

Karyn Parsons as Hilary Banks on *The Fresh Prince of Bel-Air*

"Vulgarity is not a sin against God, but against polite society. Between you and me, I don't give a shit about polite society."

Clancy Brown as Brother Justin Crowe on *Carnivale*

"KISS MY GRITS."

Polly Holliday as Flo on *Alice*

"Who wants to be a SKINNY PENCIL? I'm happy being a MAGIC MARKER!"

Mindy Cohn as Natalie Green on *The Facts of Life*

"Hey, I don't mind if I TOOT my own horn. Toot, toot!"

Michael J. Fox as Alex P. Keaton on *Family Ties*

"Now we do the DANCE OF JOY!"

Bronson Pinchot as Balki Bartokomous on *Perfect Strangers*

Quiz: Same Character, Different Face

Not feeling quite like yourself lately? Just consider how *Bewitched's* Darrin felt—one day he's being brought to life by lovable Dick York, and the next, by Dick Sargent. The infamous actor switcheroo has happened many times since. For each character below, can you choose the first person to step into their shoes?

1. Miss Ellie, *Dallas*
   a. Barbara Bel Geddes
   b. Donna Reed

2. Catwoman, *Batman*
   a. Eartha Kitt
   b. Julie Newmar

3. Lionel Jefferson, *The Jeffersons*
   a. Damon Evans
   b. Mike Evans

4. Gladys Kravitz, *Bewitched*
   a. Alice Pearce
   b. Sandra Gould

5. Aunt Vivian Banks, *The Fresh Prince of Bel-Air*
   a. Janet Hubert-Whitten
   b. Daphne Maxwell Reid

6. Becky Connor, *Roseanne*
   a. Sarah Chalke
   b. Lecy Goranson

7. Marilyn Munster, *The Munsters*
   a. Beverly Owen
   b. Pat Priest

Answers: 1. a 2. b 3. b 4. a 5. a 6. b 7. a

"I cannot let any man TOUCH me, TALK to me, or SEE me, or I'll be shooting out kids like a Pez dispenser."

Rhea Perlman as Carla Tortelli on *Cheers*

"I keep a list of people who touch my behind without permission. Some of them have died UNNATURAL and UNTIMELY deaths."

Dixie Carter as Julia Sugarbaker on *Designing Women*

"Dude, I know how this works. This is going to end with you and me running through the jungle... screaming, crying...he catches ME first because I'm heavy and I get cramps."

Jorge Garcia as Hurley on *Lost*

"I don't know why I should even BOTHER to eat this. I should just apply it directly to my hips."

Valerie Harper as Rhoda Morgenstern on *The Mary Tyler Moore Show*

CHAPTER 3

Hard Times

and
How to
Be a
Survivor

If television has taught us anything in recent years, it's that the real sign of success is winning money on a reality TV show. But for those of us who aren't always winners, it's important to be able to laugh at our troubles. Many of our TV friends have the benefit of the laugh track to fill in those awkward moments, like when they run into an ex, make a sarcastic comment to hide their pain, or trip and fall on their faces. Although you don't have a laugh track, remember to have a sense of humor: you'll soon find that when everyone else is laughing, you will, too.

"This next song, ladies and gentlemen, is about SUFFERING. God knows that it's something that we've all done a little bit of, and I'm gonna tell you about it tonight. I've been hurt SO MANY times, folks: four, four times."

Jonathan Katz as the voice of Dr. Katz on
Dr. Katz, Professional Therapist

"It was like a KNIFE IN HIS HEART when she stuck that fork in his back."

Kathy Najimy as the voice of Peggy Hill on *King of the Hill*

"Can you believe the INCOMPETENCE of that man! I very clearly asked for a whisper of cinnamon, and he's given me a full-throated shout! There are countries in this world where they would LOP OFF his sprinkling hand!"

David Hyde Pierce as Niles Crane on *Frasier*

"Choose the one drink you wouldn't give your worst enemy, and give me a DOUBLE."

Bruce Campbell as Autolycus on *Xena: Warrior Princess*

"You're pretty HIGH and FAR OUT. What kind of kick are you on, son?"

Jack Webb as Sgt. Joe Friday on *Dragnet*

• Life Lesson •

Television Therapy

Sometimes, there's only one way to make it through those rough patches—professional help. But finding the right therapist can be quite a difficult process, so consult your handy television to identify traits you'd prefer (or prefer to avoid) in a prospective therapist. For one, if you're put off by an analyst who just might be more neurotic than you, steer clear of the Niles Crane and Bob Hartley types. Alternatively, there's someone like Dr. Katz, of *Dr. Katz, Professional Therapist*, who psychoanalyzes some of the more disturbed minds in America: comedians. And if the doctor can handle their endless monologues, he can surely wrap you up in a neat little bow. However, if you feel you require a therapist with an even stronger will, there's only one place to turn: New Jersey. Dr. Jennifer Melfi, Tony Soprano's go-to support system, withstands great trauma of her own in the form of Tony's murderous misdeeds, sexual advances, and threats of physical abuse. It's unclear whether the mob boss makes any progress, but Dr. Melfi persists nonetheless. So next time you have trouble differentiating your Jungians from your Freudians, look instead to these TV archetypes of the psychiatric profession to better evaluate your options, and find a couch that's right for you.

"Do you think it's EASY to fail? This has taken me a considerable amount of work and energy."

Joshua Jackson as Pacey Witter on *Dawson's Creek*

"I am metaphorically curled up in the FETAL POSITION, and you continue to kick me about the ear, nose, and throat!"

Sean Hayes as Jack McFarland on *Will & Grace*

"I had no idea that humans were so RESILIENT. It's not a trait found in most primate species."

Scott MacDonald as Commander Dolim on *Star Trek: Enterprise*

"My pappy always said, 'A coward dies a THOUSAND DEATHS, a hero dies but ONE.' A thousand to one is pretty good odds."

James Garner as Bret Maverick on *Maverick*

"The supple willow does not contend against the storm, yet it survives."

Philip Ahn as Master Kan on *Kung Fu*

"Walk as though you're walking through HELL in GASOLINE-SOAKED pajamas!"

J. Alexander on *America's Next Top Model*

"You see this little hole? This moth's just about to emerge. It's in there right now, STRUGGLING. It's digging its way through the thick hide of the cocoon. Now, I could help it—take my knife, gently widen the opening, and the moth would be FREE—but it would be too weak to survive. Struggle is NATURE'S WAY of strengthening it."

Terry O'Quinn as John Locke on *Lost*

"Ah! The old 'drug his prunes, fake the fight, ransack the apartment, and switch places with the admiral' trick."

Don Adams as Maxwell Smart on *Get Smart*

"You can't have two guys feeding the same cat without SOMEBODY getting hurt."

Bill Daily as Howard Borden on *The Bob Newhart Show*

"When life keeps you in the DARK, baby, that's when you start looking at the STARS."

Della Reese as Tess on *Touched by an Angel*

"When I get upset, I kick things. When you get upset, you CHANGE THE SHELF PAPER."

Jack Klugman as Oscar Madison on *The Odd Couple*

"I'll COMPLAIN if I want to. It's comforting."

Robert Picardo as The Doctor on *Star Trek: Voyager*

"GOD'LL GET YOU FOR THAT!"

Bea Arthur as Maude Findlay on *Maude*

"That was not good enough, and if you WIN this competition, we will have failed."

Simon Cowell on *American Idol*

Quiz: Crutches

Next time you're feeling down, don't reach for that cigarette, box of Entenmann's, or *America's Next Top Model* marathon—answer these instead.

1. On *Dallas*, living with the merciless J.R. sent former Miss Texas Sue Ellen Shephard plunging off the deep end with what tragic addiction?

2. Vince Chase and his *Entourage* regularly partake of this, their best-loved pastime, without a twinge of paranoia.
   a. illegal gambling
   b. rock climbing
   c. marijuana smoking
   d. break dancing

3. In a dramatic change of character, serial overachiever Alex P. Keaton on *Family Ties* becomes so dependent on this crutch that he threatens sister Mallory out of pure desperation.

4. True or false: Man-about-the-office Chandler Bing of *Friends* alleviates work-related stress by hitting the neighborhood bar, Central Perk.

5. Rather than join the Key Club, this rich kid on the '90s teen drama *Beverly Hills, 90210* turned sports betting into his primary extracurricular activity.

6. *Saved by the Bell*'s Lisa Turtle is forced to turn Bayside High School's hallways into her own personal flea market in order to pay for her addiction to what?
   a. "pep" pills   b. shopping   c. cappuccinos   d. Chapstick

Answers: 1. alcoholism 2. c 3. diet pills 4. false (it's a coffee shop) 5. Brandon Walsh 6. b

"You know what, Brooke? Cancel my subscription, I'm over your issues."

Carly Pope as Sam McPherson on *Popular*

"We're in an ACTIVE CODE, Chloe. We don't have time for your personality disorder."

James Morrison as Bill Buchanan on *24*

"Don't call me an ALCOHOLIC because I'll snap and I'll cry, and it'll make you feel like an asshole."

Randy Barry on *The Real World: San Diego*

"My wife had left me, which was very painful. Then she came back to me, which was EXCRUCIATING."

Kelsey Grammer as Fraiser Crane on *Fraiser*

"I just want to make it clear that Brandon is no longer available to be your KNIGHT IN SHINING ARMOR. If you're having problems figuring out your life, watch DR. PHIL."

Alison Sweeney as Sami Brady on *Days of Our Lives*

"Kiss my SURPRISINGLY FIRM butt."

Doris Grau as the voice of Doris on *The Critic*

"I'm a cop and live with my parents. I'm on a CONSTANT DIET of human suffering."

Brad Garrett as Robert Barone on *Everybody Loves Raymond*

"I cried when I had no shoes, until I met a man who had no feet. And then I laughed REALLY hard."

Amy Sedaris as Jerri Blank on *Strangers with Candy*

"Boy, AMERICA'S A TOUGH TOWN."

Andy Kaufman as Latka Gravas on *Taxi*

"Whenever I get depressed, I RAISE MY HEMLINES. If things don't change, I am bound to be arrested."

Calista Flockhart as Ally McBeal on *Ally McBeal*

"Like women all over America, my mother confronted tragedy and death with COLD HAM and JELL-O SALAD."

Daniel Stern as narrator Kevin Arnold on *The Wonder Years*

"He beat me so bad I had to take the underground railroad home."

Tyler Williams as Chris on *Everybody Hates Chris*

"That skank ho poured BEER on my weave!"

Tiffany Richardson on *America's Next Top Model*

"It's all fun and games till one of you gets my foot up your ass."

Kristen Bell as Veronica Mars on *Veronica Mars*

"When you live on the streets,
you don't GO out, you ARE out."

Leonardo DiCaprio as Luke Brower on *Growing Pains*

"You know what DOG FOOD tastes like? Do you?
It tastes just like it smells: delicious."

Dave Chappelle as Tyrone Biggums on *Chappelle's Show*

Making Up Is Hard to Do

Going through a rough patch with a close friend of yours? Take heart: even the dearest of TV comrades have butted heads, and the relationship is actually benefited after the parties are able to work things through. For instance, when Rhoda Morgenstern divulges to the staff at WJM-TV that Mary lied on her job application, the two pals don't speak for a week. Will and Grace have a seemingly irreparable fight when their plans for artificial insemination are bungled by a series of obstacles (especially Grace's courtship by a strapping Jewish doctor). But with a little talking, these fights are neatly resolved by the end of the episode. Of course, sometimes it takes more than one episode to reconcile a friendship—especially when betrayal is involved. Take Pacey and Dawson of *Dawson's Creek*, whose relation-ship is destroyed when Dawson learns of Pacey's budding affair with Dawson's childhood sweetheart. In this case, the boys' reconciliation requires that fate, and perhaps Mother Nature, lend a helping hand: when Pacey's boat is threatened by a treacherous thunder-storm at sea, Dawson must come to his rescue. So, although your relationship may be sailing the stormy seas right now, take a tip from TV's best friends and talk it out, no matter how long it takes.

"Human beings are designed for many things. LONELINESS isn't one of them."

Brenda Strong as Mary Alice Young on *Desperate Housewives*

"Look at his poor, pathetic face. He's so sad he could depress RICHARD SIMMONS."

Jaleel White as Steve Urkel on *Family Matters*

"You have the right to an attorney. In the unlikely event that DADDY can't afford to buy you one, one will be provided for you."

Christopher Meloni as Det. Elliot Stabler on *Law & Order: SVU*

"Weaseling out of things is important to learn. It's what separates us from the animals...except the weasel."

Dan Castellaneta as the voice of Homer Simpson on *The Simpsons*

"I'm Jewish. That's no CAKEWALK either. Last year I was elected school treasurer. I didn't even run!"

Samm Levine as Neal Schweiber on *Freaks and Geeks*

"You're not married, you don't have a girlfriend, you live alone...and you've NEVER seen *Star Trek*? Good Lord!"

Patrick Stewart as himself on *Extras*

"Kids! Check your TV listings. Make sure this isn't the last episode!"

Lorenzo Music as the voice of Garfield on *Garfield and Friends*

"I was waiting for the universe to dispense some JUSTICE, but sometimes the universe is just too damn slow. The effects of putting Nair in someone's styling gel, however, only takes a few minutes."

Candice Bergen as Murphy Brown on *Murphy Brown*

"FATE is what you call it when you don't know the name of the person screwing you over."

Jane Kazmarek as Lois on *Malcolm in the Middle*

CHAPTER 4

Never Date a Guest Star

and Other Relationship Advice

Even if you're married to a witch or have three wives, TV has a relationship that's just like yours. Maybe you're happily married like Cliff and Claire Huxtable, begrudgingly together like Al and Peg Bundy, or secretly crushing like Ross Geller and Rachel Green. No matter what the situation, hopefully your sweetheart will be around longer than the short-lived guest star, who steals the main character's heart only to leave the show after sweeps week (or when a juicy movie part comes along). TV can teach us many more lessons about dating, from what not to wear to when to plant that kiss. So keep watching!

"I would invite you back, but I'm afraid you'll say YES."

Thaao Penghlis as Tony Dimera on *Days of Our Lives*

"Hey baby, I NOTICED YOU NOTICING ME, and I just wanted to put you on NOTICE that I NOTICED YOU, too."

Will Smith on *The Fresh Prince of Bel-Air*

"When GUYS are persistent, it's romantic, they make movies about that. If it's a WOMAN, then they cast Glenn Close."

Calista Flockhart as Ally McBeal on *Ally McBeal*

• Life Lesson •

Will You Go Out with Me?

Although TV land is filled with happy couples from Ozzie and Harriet to Chandler and Monica, if you're looking for how to ask out that special someone, TV seems to be full of examples of only what *not* to do. The first thing to remember: don't listen to your friends. Taking your pals' tips on how to pick someone up can only lead to your would-be date thinking you're crazy (like when Richie tries to pick up a girl Fonzie-style), or worse yet, you'll end up pinching the buxom bottom of your best friend's mom (like Fez on *That '70s Show*, taking some bad advice from Kelso at the Piggly Wiggly). The second rule? As tempting as it may be, don't lie. As much as *Sex and the City*'s Miranda wanted the object of her affection to think she was an airline stewardess or *Fresh Prince*'s Will wanted his prospective lady to think he was a Republican, these lies only led to trouble (albeit with some added hilarity for the viewer). In fact, TV's only positive example of how to successfully woo may come from one George Costanza, who decides he's going to act the opposite of all his impulses (in other words, he decides not to lie about everything): "My name is George. I'm unemployed, and I live with my parents." This time, the woman accepted a date immediately.

"Kate, a man who is NOT A RELATIVE wants to take me out."

Jane Curtin as Allie Lowell on *Kate & Allie*

"It turns out that I'm QUITE SKILLED at getting a date if it's not for me."

Adam Brody as Seth Cohen on *The OC*

"Big 3-0, huh? It's the perfect age. You can date college girls AND their mothers."

Alan Ruck as Stuart Bondek on *Spin City*

"Carmine and I have an understanding. I'm allowed to date OTHER GUYS, and he's allowed to date UGLY WOMEN."

Cindy Williams as Shirley Feeny on *Laverne & Shirley*

"She is the biggest bitch at West Beverly High. I should know. I WENT OUT WITH HER FOR A YEAR."

Ian Ziering as Steve Sanders on *Beverly Hills, 90210*

"Trust me, the ONLY MAN who can satisfy a woman in TWO MINUTES is COLONEL SANDERS."

Renée Taylor as Sylvia Fine on *The Nanny*

"SEX WITH AN EX can be depressing. If it's good, you don't have it anymore; if it's bad, you just had SEX WITH AN EX."

Kim Cattrall as Samantha Jones on *Sex and the City*

"Sex can lead to NASTY things like herpes, gonorrhea, and something called relationships."

Sacha Baron Cohen as Ali G on *The Ali G Show*

"We're not going anywhere until the ground rules are straight. First of all, this is not a real date. It's a 'NON-DATE.' Second, no one must ever know about this 'NON-DATE.' Third, if you touch me at any time, the 'NON-DATE' is over."

Kellie Shanygne Williams as Laura Winslow on *Family Matters*

"I've never understood the female capacity to avoid a DIRECT ANSWER to any question."

Leonard Nimoy as Mr. Spock on *Star Trek*

"Look, this is an odd question, but you're kind of cute and you're pretty nice to me. ARE YOU DRUNK? It's OK if you are."

Drew Carey on *The Drew Carey Show*

"Of all the Basic Applied Economic Principles of Capitalism in the Post-Industrial Era Seminars in the world, you had to WALK INTO MINE."

Michael J. Fox as Alex P. Keaton on *Family Ties*

"You're not the first to be deceived by my RUGGED GOOD LOOKS and boyish charm."

Erik Palladino as Dr. Dave Malucci on *ER*

"You date one woman all the time and pretty soon people start taking you for granted. They don't say, 'Let's invite ANDY,' or 'Let's invite ELLY.' No, they say, 'Let's invite ANDY and ELLY!' See, then it's 'ANDY AND ELLY'; 'ELLY AND ANDY.' And then that's when that woman gets her claws into you!"

Andy Griffith as Andy Taylor on *The Andy Griffith Show*

Quiz: The Dates of *Seinfeld*

No one has showed us the pratfalls of dating quite like the *Seinfeld* crew. Can you identify which *Seinfeld* character (Jerry, Elaine, George, or Kramer) dated each of the people below?

1. The "Close Talker"
2. Susan Ross
3. "Shmoopy"
4. Miss Rhode Island
5. The "Low Talker"
6. Delores (a.k.a. Mulva)
7. Puddy
8. The convict
9. Marisa Tomei
10. Sue Ellen Mishke
11. The lab scientist
12. Marla the Virgin

Answers:
1. Elaine 2. George 3. Jerry 4. Jerry 5. Kramer 6. Jerry 7. Elaine 8. George 9. George 10. Jerry 11. Kramer 12. Jerry

"I don't want to be HAPPY; I want to be with you."

Norman Fell as Stanley Roper on *Three's Company*

"Ever since we said 'I DO,' there have been so many things that we don't."

Lucille Ball as Lucy Ricardo on *I Love Lucy*

"Gary and I used to have sex, now we have Emma."

Patricia Kalember as Susannah Hart on *thirtysomething*

"Fez, the foundation of a good relationship is three little words: I DON'T KNOW. What're you doing? I don't know. What're you thinking about? I don't know. Who's that under you? I don't know."

Ashton Kutcher as Michael Kelso on *That '70s Show*

"I'd better call Pickles and tell her to START FIGHTING without me."

Morey Amsterdam as Buddy Sorrell on *The Dick Van Dyke Show*

"I think I'm missing the RELATIONSHIP CHROMOSOME."

Peter Horton as Prof. Gary Shepherd on *thirtysomething*

"Leo, you're a nice guy, and I like you a lot, but let's face it, you're GEOGRAPHICALLY UNDESIRABLE."

Holly Marie Combs as Piper Halliwell on *Charmed*

"If I had a nickel for EVERY TIME a girl dumped me, disappeared for five years, and CAME BACK as a guy...I'd have a nickel."

Charlie Sheen as Charlie Harper on *Two and a Half Men*

"Men can't be rushed, they're like CHICKENS. You cook 'em too fast, they get tough. Where you let 'em simmer, they fall apart in your hands."

Fran Drescher as Fran Fine on *The Nanny*

"That's your idea of a ROMANTIC DINNER, Oscar? Red wine and fish sticks?"

Tony Randall as Felix Unger on *The Odd Couple*

"Now I have to go back and ARREST MY GIRLFRIEND for conspiracy and attempted murder. She'll probably break up with me!"

Jason Gray-Stanford as Lt. Randall Disher on *Monk*

"In a courtroom, REASONABLE DOUBT can get you off for murder. In an engagement, it makes you feel like a bad person."

Cynthia Nixon as Miranda Hobbes on *Sex and the City*

• Life Lesson •

Making a Graceful Exit

Breaking up is hard to do...especially when you're the one doing the breaking. Rule number one: be honest. But, in case your soon-to-be-ex still refuses to believe the romance is over, look to some of the more impressive breakup tactics on your favorite television shows. There's always the "reaching-for-my-dreams" excuse—like Diane Chambers on *Cheers*, who deserted Sam at the altar to pursue a career as a novelist. Classics like "it's not you, it's me" and "I love you, but I'm not 'in love' with you" are reused so incessantly that no one actually believes them anymore. Be creative! If you're planning to fib your way out of the relationship, think your white lies through so they don't come back to irk you in the future. Think before you get yourself into a real pickle. For example, do justify your philandering ways with a devastatingly chronic sex addiction, like Brenda on *Six Feet Under*. Don't make like Chandler Bing and tell your future ex that you're up-and-moving to Yemen. You wouldn't want to end up on a plane to a Middle Eastern country while your poor unsuspecting girlfriend gazes adoringly out the airport window.

"The world is made up of two kinds of people, TWOS and ONES. Sometimes two ONES become a TWO, and other times one of the ONES of the two gets tired of being a TWO and wants to become a ONE again, not that the other one of the TWO isn't a nice one, it's just that two ONES can't be a TWO without the ONE. See?"

Suzanne Somers as Chrissy Snow on *Three's Company*

"If you, like, make out with a frog, then YOU TURN INTO PRINCE."

Mike Judge as the voice of Butt-head on *Beavis and Butt-head*

"You just have to give guys a chance. Sometimes you meet a guy and think he's a pig, but then later on you realize he actually has a REALLY GOOD BODY."

Lauren Tom as the voice of Amy Wong on *Futurama*

"Why do you have to break up with her? Be a man. Just STOP CALLING."

Matt LeBlanc as Joey Tribbiani on *Friends*

"First divorce: wife's hidden sexuality, NOT MY FAULT. Second divorce: said the wrong name at the altar, KIND OF MY FAULT."

David Schwimmer as Ross Geller on *Friends*

"Divorce is very difficult, especially on the kids. OF COURSE, I'm the result of my parents having stayed together, so you never know."

Jason Alexander as George Costanza on *Seinfeld*

CHAPTER 5

The Office,

Where Everyone Knows Your Name

Just as every show needs a setting (preferably a radio station or a hospital), you need somewhere where you can meet up with friends, spar with enemies, and get yourself into ridiculous situations. As much as you may loathe your job, ask yourself: where else would I get the fodder for the hilarity of my everyday life? Jobs not only help us relate to the characters onscreen, but to the people around us as well.

"You know those nature shows where a wasp paralyzes a caterpillar, then injects it full of larvae? It stays ALIVE for weeks, completely aware, feeling every little bite as the larvae DEVOUR it from the inside. I sat in a cubicle every day ENVYING that caterpillar, because at least he got to be on TV."

Bryan Cranston as Hal on *Malcolm in the Middle*

"One thing about being a CABBIE is that you don't have to worry about being fired from a good job."

Judd Hirsch as Alex Rieger on *Taxi*

"I always did want to be a bar-
ber...I used to practice on cats.
We had the BALDEST CATS in the
county."

Howard McNear as Floyd Lawson on *The Andy Griffith Show*

"Sally, I'm a COP. I've got keen instincts. And right
now, my instincts are telling me that...I don't know
what the hell is going on."

Wayne Knight as Officer Don on *3rd Rock from the Sun*

"You girls can't eat here. You're WAITRESSES, not people."

Vic Tayback as Mel Sharples on *Alice*

"I'm hoping to open up a little restaurant for people who can REALLY APPRECIATE high prices."

John Ritter as Jack Tripper on *Three's Company*

"I hope he doesn't rush too much SHUCKING the oysters, or he might SHUCK his hand off. That would be a SHUCKING tragedy."

Ted Allen on *Queer Eye for the Straight Guy*

"Ed and I drove around for hours for NO PARTICULAR REASON. We came up empty."

Leslie Nielsen as Det. Frank Drebin on *Police Squad!*

"Come on, don't you guys have some gizmo to track this thing? That blue light with the buzzers and bells or that MASS-SPECTRO-DETECTO-WHATEVER-YOU-CALL-IT thingy?"

Rex Linn as Det. Frank Tripp on *CSI: Miami*

"I have killed two people since midnight. I haven't slept in over 24 HOURS. So maybe you should be a little more afraid of me than you are now."

Kiefer Sutherland as Jack Bauer on *24*

"Being a SLAYER is not the same as being a KILLER."

Sarah Michelle Gellar as Buffy Summers on *Buffy the Vampire Slayer*

"I've never worked in a FUNERAL HOME that was more depressing."

Illeana Douglas as Angela on *Six Feet Under*

"OF COURSE I believe in evil—I work in real estate."

Nicollette Sheridan as Edie Britt on *Desperate Housewives*

"I'll keep it short and sweet—FAMILY. RELIGION. FRIENDSHIP. These are the three demons you must slay if you wish to succeed in business."

Harry Shearer as the voice of Montgomery Burns on *The Simpsons*

Quiz: Which Workplace?

Work is not only where we learn and grow, but where we spend most of our time. Many television shows used the workplace as a jumping off point for friendships, relationships, and adding a little humor to life. Match the fictional company on the left with the show on which it was featured on the right.

1. Sunshine
2. Blush
3. WJM-TV
4. WNYX Radio
5. KACL Radio
6. Dunder-Mifflin
7. Salinger's restaurant
8. County General Hospital
9. Blair General Hospital
10. The Peach Pit
11. Fisher & Diaz
12. Strickland Propane

a. *Frasier*
b. *The Mary Tyler Moore Show*
c. *ER*
d. *Beverly Hills, 90210*
e. *King of the Hill*
f. *Taxi*
g. *The Office*
h. *Just Shoot Me*
i. *Dr. Kildare*
j. *NewsRadio*
k. *Six Feet Under*
l. *Party of Five*

Answers: 1. f, 2. h, 3. b, 4. j, 5. a, 6. g, 7. l, 8. c, 9. i, 10. d, 11. k, 12. e

"If you can't DRINK THEIR BOOZE, TAKE THEIR MONEY, and then VOTE AGAINST THEM, then you're in the wrong business."

Alan Alda as Sen. Arnold Vinick on *The West Wing*

"Here's the thing. CHILI'S is the new golf course. It's where business happens. *Small Business Man* magazine."

Steve Carrell as Michael Scott on *The Office*

"I gave *The Sacred and the Sinful* the best years of my life, and how do they repay me? With a cheesy EVIL TWIN MURDER-SUICIDE!"

Kelly Ripa (about being written off her soap opera) on *Hope & Faith*

"Overton, it's not right to let people WALK ALL OVER YOU. Unless that someone employs you, and gives you a place to stay. Then you just don't have a choice."

Kim Coles as Synclaire James on *Living Single*

"You have your finance person and you have your team leader, and the money DISAPPEARED some-where between the hand and the ass. Right?"

Donald Trump on *The Apprentice*

"Discussing STRATEGY with you would be like playing chess with a sugar bowl."

Constance Towers as Helena Cassadine on *General Hospital*

"Give a LAZY man a job, and he'll find a LAZY way to do it."

Roy Rogers on *The Roy Rogers Show*

Who's in Charge Here?

Whether your supervisor is superrich, like *Newsradio*'s Jimmy James and *Just Shoot Me*'s Jack Gallo, or superbitch like *ER*'s Dr. Weaver and *Desperate Housewives*' Nina Fletcher, one thing's for sure: you could have it worse. You could have a boss like many of your friends in TV Land, who are all but terrorized by bungling bosses. Dr. Bailey on *Grey's Anatomy*, for instance, works her interns to the bone by giving them the worst tasks possible during their 48-hour shifts. And President Logan on *24* makes it a very long day for his employee Jack Bauer when he indirectly engineers the selling of toxic nerve gas to Chechen terrorists. Remember, it's better to have a superior who's lovably surly like *Mary Tyler Moore*'s Lou Grant than someone who's just downright mean like *Taxi*'s Louie DePalma (although Louie is always suspiciously easy to bully). And if *The Office* has taught us anything, it's that there's one kind of boss that's the worst of all: the boss who thinks he's funny. Just ask the employees of Wernham Hogg, setting of the original British *Office*. As their commander in chief David Brent says, "I've created an atmosphere where I'm a friend first, boss second. Probably entertainer third." If only!

"New York is a RAT RACE, and the rats are WINNING."

Eddie Albert as Oliver Wendell Douglas on *Green Acres*

"Never combine BUSINESS with PLEASURE; that's not good business."

Judge Judy Sheindlin on *Judge Judy*

"I know you've got to fill your column, but if you fill it with crap, you end up with what we call in the business a CRAP COLUMN."

Jeffrey Tambor as Hank Kingsley on *The Larry Sanders Show*

"Sometimes I get concerned about being a CAREER WOMAN. I get to thinking that my job is too important to me. And I tell myself that the people I work with are just the people I work with. But last night I thought what is family anyway? It's the people who make you feel less alone and really loved."

Mary Tyler Moore as Mary Richards on *The Mary Tyler Moore Show*

"GEE, your kitchen always looks so clean. My mother says it looks as though you never do any work in here."

Ken Osmond as Eddie Haskell on *Leave It to Beaver*

"Where's a GOOD HOMICIDE when you need one?"

Rick Schroder as Det. Danny Sorenson on *NYPD Blue*

"We're sorry to bother you at such a time like this, Mrs. Twice. We would have come earlier, but your husband wasn't dead then."

Leslie Nielsen as Det. Frank Drebin on *Police Squad!*

"We have two passes to be witnesses at an execution. I know we all want these, so we're gonna do this the way we generally handle these things, and we're gonna have a SCAVENGER HUNT."

Thomas Lennon as Lt. Jim Dangle on *Reno 911!*

"Oh, good morning, my little worker ants! That's just a figure of speech; I would never compare you to insects. At least not after that SENSITIVITY TRAINING seminar those maggots at the network forced me to attend!"

Lily Tomlin as Kay Carter-Shepley on *Murphy Brown*

"I don't think it would be the WORST THING IN THE WORLD if they let me go. Because then I might...it's just...I don't think many girls grow up wanting to be a receptionist."

Jenna Fischer as Pam Beesly on *The Office*

Life Lesson

Sometimes You Just Need a Vacation

Revving up for a long-overdue vacation? Remember, a trip away from home will always lead to shenanigans (if TV has taught us anything). So unless you want spend your entire holiday wedged in bumper-to-bumper traffic like the Bundys or on a wild-goose chase for 27th-century weapons like Jean-Luc Picard, follow these tips. First, don't forget to check those weather reports! If Lucy Ricardo had only checked the weather before heading into the Swiss Alps, her famous foursome could have avoided the snowstorm that left them trapped under an avalanche. Foreign currency can get complicated, too. Refrain from folding your last million yen into an origami crane on a windy day like Homer Simpson, who had to withstand the physical torture of the Japanese game show *The Happy Smile Super Challenge Family Wish Show* to win plane tickets back to Springfield. And finally, stay away from tikis, which led the Bradys into such a string of bad luck on their Hawaiian getaway that Greg almost drowned! With these tips, your vacation will be the perfect way to spend those "on-location" episodes of your life. And if you hit some bumps along the way and need some cash, be confident that game shows, eating contests, and talent competitions exist in all corners of the planet.

"Isn't this great, Squidward? Just you and me together for HOURS and HOURS and HOURS! And then the sun'll come up, and it'll be tomorrow, and we'll still be working! It'll be just like a sleepover! Only we'll be sweaty and covered with grease!"

Tom Kenny as the voice of Spongebob Squarepants (on working the night shift) on *Spongebob Squarepants*

"I have a full-grown, SEMINUDE man bound with duct tape in my truck and I was trying to get out to the desert to bury him. How do I get to 5 South?"

Johnny Knoxville on *Jackass*

"I'm an Air Force officer just like you are, Colonel. And just because my reproductive organs are on the INSIDE instead of the OUTSIDE doesn't mean I can't handle whatever you can handle."

Amanda Tapping as Capt. Samantha Carter on *Star Gate: SG-1*

"Okay, people. Let's set up for the birthday greetings. I've got a network note here: SUSIE and KENNY are now SHANIQUA and CARLOS."

Eugene Levy as Gil Bender on *Greg the Bunny*

"I want my employees to show some INITIATIVE, but only when I tell them to."

Jill Marie Jones as Toni Childs on *Girlfriends*

"I'm going to make a suggestion which might help you out, but I don't want this to be mistaken for an indication that I LIKE YOU."

Richard Schiff as Toby Ziegler on *The West Wing*

"Oh, you hate your job? Why didn't you say so? There's a support group for that. It's called EVERYBODY, and they meet at the bar."

Drew Carey on *The Drew Carey Show*

"Freedom is irrelevant. RESISTANCE IS FUTILE. Prepare to be assimilated."

The Borg on *Star Trek: The Next Generation*

CHAPTER 6

Your Friends and Family

(and Other Co-Stars)

They'll be there for you...whether you want them to or not. On TV shows, it's not always so easy to kick out a misbehaving actor or actress, and the same holds true for your own "co-stars." So whether it's a best friend, a bratty nephew, or even a sworn enemy who's giving you trouble, remember that writing someone out of the script of your life may be more difficult than learning to deal with them. Get along with the people around you, and if you can't, at least make sure to make up at the end of the episode.

"My pa always said EVERY MAN is your friend until he shows you otherwise."

Dan Blocker as Hoss Cartwright on *Bonanza*

"Once you're into THIS FAMILY, there's no getting out."

James Gandolfini as Tony Soprano on *The Sopranos*

"I would take a BULLET for my grandson, but not in the face. That's how I makes my livings."

Toby Huss as the voice of Cotton Hill on *King of the Hill*

"Humans have got such LIMITED LITTLE MINDS. I don't know why I like you so much."

Tom Baker as The Doctor on *Doctor Who*

"I've never felt closer to a group of people. Not even in the PORTABLE JOHNS of Woodstock."

Christopher Lloyd as Rev. Jim Ignatowski on *Taxi*

"When we're at a U2 concert, you are my BEST FRIEND. But right now you are my sixteen-year-old daughter."

Lauren Graham as Lorelai Gilmore on *Gilmore Girls*

"Keith, that's the MEANEST, ROTTENEST, and DIRTIEST trick anyone can play on his sister. No wonder you're my IDOL!"

Danny Bonaduce as Danny Partridge on *The Partridge Family*

"I'm Larry. This is my brother Darryl, and this is my other brother Darryl."

William Sanderson as Larry on *Newhart*

Quiz: All About *Friends*

Whether it's to boost our spirits or boost our ratings, it's nice to have *Friends* around. How well do you know these *Friends* facts?

1. Which of Ross's ex-girlfriends was never at one point married to Ross?

   a. Emily   b. Julie   c. Rachel   d. Carol

2. True or false: A record producer offers singer/songwriter/masseuse Phoebe the opportunity to film a music video for her song, "My Stinky Shoe."

3. Joey Tribbiani plays Dr. Drake Ramore on *Days of Our Lives*. Which *Friends* star has a father who's a real-life actor on that very same program?

4. When she discovers that her estranged evil twin, Ursula, is using Phoebe's name in a prolific adult film career, Phoebe is understandably infuriated. Which of the following film titles is not one of Ursula's films?

   a. *Sex Toy Story 2*   b. *Lawrence of Alabia*

   c. *Monkeywench*   d. *Buffay the Vampire Layer*

5. True or false: Chandler Bing has the unfortunate middle name "Muriel."

6. Which of the following couples never locked lips during the series' run?

   a. Rachel and Joey   b. Phoebe and Ross

   c. Monica and Joey   d. Rachel and Phoebe

Answers:

1. b 2. false (the name of the song is "Smelly Cat") 3. Jennifer Aniston's father, John, plays Victor 4. c 5. true 6. c

"Everything changes eventually. That's just the way life is, and you have no control over it. Like suddenly people who you think are always going to be there, they DISAPPEAR. People die and they move away and they grow up."

Katie Holmes as Joey Potter on *Dawson's Creek*

"I have never understood why people are TOO PROUD to take money from friends. They will accept the things that are HARDEST to give: friends will accept your time, your tears, your patience, and your love—so why is it so hard to take a few dollars?"

Dixie Carter as Julia Sugarbaker on *Designing Women*

"I am your FATHER. I brought you into this world—
and I can take you out!"

Bill Cosby as Cliff Huxtable on *The Cosby Show*

"The only fathers that don't YELL AT THEIR KIDS are
on television."

Tony Dow as Wally Cleaver on *Leave It to Beaver*

"In my experience, when a father and son don't get
along it usually means they've got EVERYTHING in
common."

Debra Mooney as Edna Wallace on *Everwood*

"Don't FORGIVE and never FORGET; do unto others BEFORE they do unto you; and third and most importantly, keep your eye on your FRIENDS, because your enemies will take care of themselves."

Larry Hagman as J.R. Ewing on *Dallas*

"From now on if we have any BACKSTABBING to do we're going to do it the way we have always done it: FACE TO FACE."

Vicki Lawrence as Thelma "Mama" Harper on *Mama's Family*

"I feel a wave of morning sickness coming on, and I want to be standing on your MOTHER'S GRAVE when it hits."

Eva Longoria as Gabrielle Solis on *Desperate Housewives*

"NOBODY knows me here! I could be ANYBODY. I could be SOMEBODY!"

Shannen Doherty as Brenda Walsh on *Beverly Hills, 90210*

"Last time I made a bet with a rich friend, oh yeah, heh, I ended up STREAKING through the Chicago Mercantile Exchange at noon."

Stephen Root as Jimmy James on *NewsRadio*

"The food was TERRIBLE, the music STINKS, the drinks were watered down, but you sure know how to throw a PARTY."

Laura Innes as Dr. Kerry Weaver on *ER*

• Life Lesson •

Man's Best Friend

If you're hankering for some more love in your life, why not consider acquiring a furry friend? Pets are wonderful sources of companionship and affection. Whether hairy, scaly, or feathered, a pet will make your home happier and more comforting by providing a reprieve from the hassles and chaos of the outside world. Take plainclothes cop Tony Baretta and his beloved cockatoo, Fred, who squawks "Freeze!" whenever Tony walks through the door. Pets also make ideal sidekicks and best friends, like Maximillion, the bionic German shepherd adopted by Jaime Sommers on the *Bionic Woman* and Flicka the horse of *My Friend Flicka*. Additionally, animals tend to be incredibly loyal and are good judges of character. Sabrina wouldn't be able to get by without the sensibilities of her talking cat, Salem. And Eddie, Martin Crane's Jack Russell terrier on *Frasier*, is devoted to Martin yet suspicious of Frasier, one of the more neurotic characters on television. While they may cause trouble from time to time—like Marcel the monkey on *Friends*, who poops in Monica's shoe and, later, loses control of his libido—pets have the ability to bring families together and to fill homes with unconditional love.

"Al didn't smile for forty years. You've got to ADMIRE a man like that."

Louise Lasser as Mary Hartman on *Mary Hartman, Mary Hartman*

"Christina, I like you, I really do. But I grew up in a TRAILER PARK and I am not above kicking your pampered little BEVERLY HILLS ass. And I do mean physically KICKING YOUR ASS."

Katherine Heigl as Dr. Izzie Stevens on *Grey's Anatomy*

"You don't kiss your FRIEND'S MOM. Sisters are okay, maybe a hot-lookin' aunt, but not a mom."

Matt LeBlanc as Joey Tribbiani on *Friends*

"So I'm licking jelly off of my boyfriend, right? And I'm thinking, EW, I'm turning into my mother."

Wendy Traston as herself on *The Larry Sanders Show*

"Kids should not be blamed for how TERRIBLE their parents are. I mean, if Saddam Hussein had a son—well, maybe that's not the best example."

Frankie Muniz as Malcolm on *Malcolm in the Middle*

"Mom liked YOU best."

Tommy Smothers (to Dick Smothers)
on *The Smothers Brothers Comedy Hour*

Quiz: Best (TV) Dad Ever

Get over your father issues by answering these questions about TV's famous pops.

1. One of TV's most beloved dads, Dr. Cliff Huxtable of *The Cosby Show*, has how many children?

   a. six   b. five   c. four   d. three

2. The Bradfords of *Eight Is Enough* are based on a true-life family. Both the fictional and the real dads have the same occupation—what?

   a. gym teacher   b. writer   c. lumberman   d. insurance agent

3. George Lopez is constantly trying to get the truth out of this family member:

   a. 16-year-old daughter Carmen   b. mother Benny

   c. wife Angie   d. 13-year-old son Max

4. Mr. Fix-It Dad Tim Taylor on *Home Improvement* is a television personality by day. What is the name of his show-within-a-show?

   a. *Home Improvement*   b. *Fixin' Fun*   c. *Tool Time*   d. *Tool-Time Taylor*

5. Of the patriarchs below, which of the following is not a widower with three children?

   a. Steve Douglas of *My Three Sons*   b. Ben Cartwright of *Bonanza*

   c. Danny Tanner of *Full House*   d. Andy Brown of *Everwood*

Answers: 1. b 2. a 3. b 4. c 5. d

"The most important thing in life is your FAMILY. There are days you LOVE them, and others you don't. But, in the end, they're the people you always come home to. Sometimes it's the family you're BORN INTO and sometimes it's the one you MAKE for yourself."

Sarah Jessica Parker as Carrie Bradshaw on *Sex and the City*

CHAPTER 7

Love,

the Greatest Ratings Boost

The sun is shining, hearts are in your eyes, and an upbeat song is in your head. You're in love! And just as our favorite shows get better ratings when their characters get together, your rating of your life will go through the roof when you find that special someone. But don't spend all your time having picnics and kissing at the movies: there are still plenty of lessons to be learned in front of the tube, from what to do on your first date to how to behave while walking down the aisle.

"I love you all. I love you more than life itself. But you're all BLEEPing mad."

Ozzy Osbourne on *The Osbournes*

"You know I love you. And you know there's only ONE THING in the world I love more than you...the thing that you're interested in borrowing."

Jonathan Katz as the voice of Dr. Katz
on *Dr. Katz, Professional Therapist*

"Well, I could try to pay the phone bill with LOVE, but I think it's a felony."

Jenna Elfman as Dharma Finkelstein-Montgomery
on *Dharma & Greg*

• Life Lesson •

Keep Pining

Are you still pining for that special someone after years of secret glances, flirty banter, and hushed declarations of affection? Well, look no further than your favorite TV shows for encouragement: the number one rule in TV romance states that if you pine long enough, your love will eventually be reciprocated (usually during sweeps week). From Major Nelson and Jeannie on *I Dream of Jeannie* to Luke and Lorelai on *Gilmore Girls*, nothing is more frustrating (or exciting) than the "will they or won't they" conundrum. And when they finally cave in to their feelings, everything clicks, stars align, and sparks fly. It took six grueling years for *Fraiser*'s Niles Crane to finally reveal his long-held flame for Daphne—and this confession is only brought to light by brother Frasier's tranquilizer-induced ramblings. Likewise, Ross Geller on *Friends* had been lusting after Rachel Green since high school—and the two went on to become one of TV's most famous couples. And of course, *Who's the Boss*'s Tony Micelli and Angela Bower, who played house for a decade, finally take a chance and face the wind when they consummate their long-overdue boss-employee romance in a local carnival's Tunnel of Love. Clearly, true love is worth the wait.

"You know, boys, a nuclear reactor is a lot like a woman. You just have to READ THE MANUAL and press the right buttons."

Dan Castellaneta as the voice of Homer Simpson on *The Simpsons*

"Why is a woman in love like a welder? Because they both carry a torch!"

Adam West as Batman on *Batman*

"One woman's TITANIC is another woman's LOVE BOAT."

Sarah Jessica Parker as Carrie Bradshaw on *Sex and the City*

"School is a BATTLEFIELD for your heart—you're lucky to get out alive."

Claire Danes as Angela Chase on *My So-Called Life*

"Let me explain something to you. I'm your MOTHER, and in that way I'll always belong to all of you. But I'm also a WOMAN. And even with five children whom I love very much, and who I know love me, there are times when I still feel lonely."

Shirley Jones as Shirley Partridge on *The Partridge Family*

"LAW and LOVE are the same—romantic in concept, but the actual practice can give you a yeast infection."

Calista Flockhart as Ally McBeal on *Ally McBeal*

"Maybe love's like MATH. You don't get better at it, but you just get used to it. Simple equations with the occasional variable."

Emily VanCamp as Amy Abbott on *Everwood*

"We have a saying in Germany. It is better to have loved and LOST than to engage in a LAND WAR with RUSSIA in the winter."

Heidi Klum as herself on *Spin City*

"Ah, c'mon, Lois, isn't 'BRIBE' just another word for 'LOVE'?"

Seth McFarlane as the voice of Peter Griffin on *Family Guy*

"You can't just WALK into my life, HAND me a package, tell me to give it to the MAN IN THE RED HAT, tell me you LOVE me, and then WALK out again!"

Kate Jackson as Amanda King on *Scarecrow and Mrs. King*

"I know what LOVE is, 'cause I watch talk shows. Love is the end of happiness!"

Danny DeVito as Louie DePalma on *Taxi*

• Life Lesson •

Save the Date

Sometimes, the most romantic dates are those that don't go exactly as planned—whether you arrange something romantic à la Dobie Gillis, or decide to up and exchange nuptials on your very first day together like Dharma Finklestein and Greg Montgomery. Be flexible, and remember that "bad" dates can sometimes turn into the best dates. Take the doomed first date of Brenda Walsh and Dylan McKay of *90210*, during which Dylan's criminal father triggers an emotional freak-out that only brings the couple closer together. Or consider the first formal date for Drs. Yang and Burke of *Grey's Anatomy*. Stony silence turns into breathtaking action as a fellow diner collapses and needs medical attention. As long as you can improvise and be yourself, you'll be able to turn any mishaps in your favor. Just ask Buffy, who is excited to finally be able to take a day off from slaying to go on a date with her crush, Owen. When the two unexpectedly end up at a morgue fighting vampires, Buffy is surprised to find Owen thrilled by all the danger. As long as you don't inadvertently handcuff yourself to your voluptuous roommate on the eve of the big date, like Jack Tripper did on *Three's Company*, if you're with the right person, you can make any encounter the most romantic date of your life.

"For a kiss to be REALLY GOOD, you want it to mean something. You want it to be with someone you can't get out of your head, so that when your lips finally touch you feel it EVERYWHERE. A kiss SO HOT and SO DEEP you never want to come up for air. You can't cheat your first kiss. Trust me, you don't want to. Because when you find that right person for a first kiss, it's EVERYTHING."

Justin Chambers as Dr. Alex Karev on *Grey's Anatomy*

"I love hotel rooms—BODY FLUIDS everywhere."

Rory Cochrane as Tim Speedle on *CSI: Miami*

"You know, for someone who loves their children SO MUCH, you certainly seem to do them a terrible disservice."

John Aniston as Victor Kiriakis on *Days of Our Lives*

"DR. WEAVER and the SOUND OF HER OWN VOICE: a love story."

George Clooney as Dr. Doug Ross on *ER*

"I don't even know what we do, really, besides clean up and complain and wish we were sleeping, but with you somehow it's FUN!"

Helen Hunt as Jamie Buchman on *Mad About You*

"When someone sees you as you REALLY ARE and wants to be with you, that's powerful."

Mathew St. Patrick as Keith Charles on *Six Feet Under*

Quiz: The Big Day

Nothing quite seals the deal like walking down the aisle. Good for a relationship and for the ratings, weddings are always an event to remember. How much do you remember about TV's most famous weddings?

1. *General Hospital*'s power couple, Luke and Laura, married in one of the grandest spectacles in the history of television. Which legendary silver screen vixen requested a small role in the day's festivities? (Hint: she crashed the wedding and placed a curse on the lovebirds.)

2. True or false: On the finale of *Happy Days*, Joanie and Chachi's wedding is performed by Howard Cunningham.

3. Which of the following events did NOT take place at Woody and Kelly's wedding on *Cheers*?

   a. the priest dies
   b. Lillith sings show tunes
   c. Rebecca and Sam sleep together
   d. someone brandishes a gun at Sam

4. True or false: On Jeannie and Major Nelson's wedding day on *I Dream of Jeannie*, Jeannie remembers that genies can never be photographed. The two spend the entire day avoiding all cameras.

5. On *Friends*, Ross's marriage to Emily is doomed from the start when he accidentally does what at the wedding?

Answers: 1. Elizabeth Taylor 2. false 3. c 4. a 5. true 5. says "Rachel" instead of "Emily"

"When you love somebody, you're always in trouble. There's only two things you can do about it: either STOP loving 'em, or love 'em A WHOLE LOT MORE."

Harry Morgan as Col. Sherman Potter on M*A*S*H

"Presents are the best way to show someone how much you care. It is like this tangible thing that you can point to and say, 'HEY MAN, I LOVE YOU THIS MANY DOLLARS' WORTH.'"

Steve Carrell as Michael Scott on The Office

"Will, my LOVE for you is like this SCAR: ugly, but permanent."

Debra Messing as Grace Adler on Will & Grace

CHAPTER 8

Self-Reflection

(With or Without Watching Reruns)

From Doogie Howser's computer journal to Meredith Grey's existential narration, nothing helps add meaning to a television show like a little self-reflection. We should all strive to rerun the trials, successes, and foibles of our own lives to see what we can learn from them. If that doesn't work, try watching your TV favorites to gain a little insight. Because there's a little Doogie and Meredith, and even Kramer and Gilligan, in all of us.

"Well, guess what, Junior? You're from the MEAN STREETS of Stamford, Connecticut."

Damon Wayans as Michael Kyle on *My Wife and Kids*

"Hey, I may LOATHE myself, but it has NOTHING to do with the fact that I'm Jewish!"

Larry David on *Curb Your Enthusiasm*

"I'm half ITALIAN and half DRAG QUEEN. I'm allowed to get worked up!"

Hal Sparks as Michael Novotny on *Queer as Folk*

"There is a FINE line between flirting and being a wanton slut. I know. My toe has been ON that line."

Rue McClanahan as Blanche Devereaux on *The Golden Girls*

"True, I'm not what you would call a WILD WOMAN. Well, alright, I might not have been around...but I've been nearby."

Mary Tyler Moore as Mary Richards on *The Mary Tyler Moore Show*

"The last mosquito that bit me had to book into the BETTY FORD CLINIC."

Joanna Lumley as Patsy Stone on *Absolutely Fabulous*

• Life Lesson •

Dear Diary

One of the most effective methods of self-analysis is putting pen to paper and recording your feelings. Take Doogie Howser, M.D., for instance, who spends the final minutes of each day typing away in his computer diary—reflecting upon stressful experiences and lessons learned as a fourteen-year-old medical doctor and an otherwise typical adolescent boy. Journal writing should be a part of your regular regimen in your quest to better understand the complexities of life, but it may grow to be an impetus for you aspiring authors out there. Serial diary-writer Mr. Belvedere—a refined English house-keeper/nanny employed by the middle-class Owens family in subur-ban Pennsylvania—hopes to turn his nightly digests into a novel. So does John Boy Walton, who details his thoughts on family and life on Walton's Mountain. Remember, diaries need not be handwritten scribbles in a lined notebook: not only is there Doogie's high-tech journaling method, but Blossom Russo records her entries on videotape, and Judy Jetson discloses her innermost thoughts to DiDi, her digital confidante. Once you find a method that's comfortable for you, gather your thoughts and dive in: a healthy dose of self-reflection will do a body good.

"I'm not proud of everything I've done. I'm not proud of having a POOR EDUCATION. I'm not proud of being DYSLEXIC. I'm not proud of being an ALCOHOLIC DRUG ADDICT. I'm not proud of BITING THE HEAD OFF A BAT. I'm not proud of having ATTENTION DEFICIT DISORDER. But I'm a real guy. To be Ozzy Osbourne, IT COULD BE WORSE. I could be Sting."

Ozzy Osbourne on *The Osbournes*

"Sometimes, when you want to BELIEVE so badly, you end up looking too hard."

Gillian Anderson as Dana Scully on *The X-Files*

"When you do EVERYTHING you can, sometimes MORE then you thought you could, you've got to walk away knowing you FOUGHT the good fight."

Noah Wyle as Dr. John Carter on *ER*

"Sometimes, you can make no mistakes, do everything right, and still LOSE."

Patrick Stewart as Capt. Jean-Luc Picard on *Star Trek: The Next Generation*

"My hormones don't rage. Oh sure, they get MAD sometimes, but then they just stop speaking to each other."

Tracy Grandstaff as the voice of Daria Morgendorffer on *Daria*

"There's an expiration date stamped on my eggs: 'Best if used before you start LOOKING LIKE YOUR MOTHER.'"

Fran Drescher as Fran Fine on *The Nanny*

"We all have to live with our disappointments... I have to SLEEP with mine."

Ed O'Neill as Al Bundy on *Married...with Children*

"I hate broccoli, and yet, in a certain sense, I AM BROCCOLI."

Townsend Coleman as the voice of The Tick on *The Tick*

"I just came in here to check my hair. PERFECT, as usual."

Henry Winkler as Arthur "the Fonz" Fonzarelli on *Happy Days*

"For the record, I really like having a penis."

Eric Szmanda as Greg Sanders on *CSI: Crime Scene Investigation*

"I LAUGH in the face of danger, then I RUN AND HIDE until it goes away."

Nicholas Brendon as Xander Harris on *Buffy the Vampire Slayer*

"I mean, you ask anybody that knows me well, and they'll tell you voluntarily that Nat, Nat is a LOVER OF ALL CREATURES, great and small. 'Nat would not harm a gnat' is a joke I enjoy making."

Hank Azaria as Nat on *Mad About You*

"So, what separates us from the rest of the animal kingdom? What makes us so different? We're the only species who put our OWN KIND in cages."

Harold Perrineau Jr. as Augustus Hill on *Oz*

"All we are, basically, are MONKEYS with CAR KEYS."

Sparkle as Grandma Woody on *Northern Exposure*

"My shrink was right! God DOES hate me!"

Jon Lovitz as the voice of Jay Sherman on *The Critic*

"Boy, I sure feel like a MARY without a Peter and a Paul."

David Cross as Tobias Funke on *Arrested Development*

"The first thing I remember liking that LIKED ME BACK was food."

Valerie Harper as Rhoda Morgenstern on *Rhoda*

"All I do is think and blink."

Barbara Eden as Jeannie on *I Dream of Jeannie*

Quiz: Mirror, Mirror

Don't go overboard...sometimes there's a fine line between self-reflection and self-absorption. Can you answer these questions about the most self-obsessed TV characters of all time?

1. Which *Golden* girl had all records of her birthdate destroyed, so no one would ever know her true age?

2. Fashion-obsessed Patsy Stone boozed and slept her way to a cushy position at a high-end fashion magazine on what cult UK comedy?

3. The outrageously narcissistic Austrian-born fashion reporter Bruno is one of the many alter egos of this cable show's host, who has interviewed the likes of Gore Vidal, Andy Rooney, Pat Buchanan, and Ralph Nader.

4. Hilary Banks, Will Smith's snotty, dim-witted cousin on *The Fresh Prince of Bel-Air*, eventually gets a job in television as what?

5. On *Arrested Development*, which Segway-riding ex-stripper and founder of the Magician's Alliance is arguably the most narcissistic family member of the shamelessly self-absorbed Bluth clan?

6. At *The Facts of Life*'s Eastland Academy, which blonde beauty queen flaunts her parents' cash and designer clothes to the annoyance of her schoolmates?

Answers: 1. Blanche Devereaux 2. *Absolutely Fabulous* 3. *Da Ali G Show* 4. a weather girl 5. GOB Bluth 6. Blair Warner

"I just feel like a big loser. I couldn't chug BEER in college, and I couldn't chug BLOOD today."

Kelly Wiglesworth on *Survivor*

"I hate when I'm an idiot and I don't know it. I like to be AWARE of my idiocy, to really revel in it, take pictures."

Lauren Graham as Lorelai Gilmore on *Gilmore Girls*

"No one can pull the wool over my eyes. CASHMERE maybe, but wool, never."

Jim Backus as Thurston Howell III on *Gilligan's Island*

"I don't like talking to people I know, but STRANGERS I have no problem with."

Larry David on *Curb Your Enthusiasm*

"Everyone thinks I'm a HYPOCHONDRIAC. It makes me sick."

Tony Randall as Felix Unger on *The Odd Couple*

"When I dance, people think I'm looking for my keys."

Ray Romano as Ray Barone on *Everybody Loves Raymond*

• Life Lesson •

When Cousins Are Two of a Kind

Nothing makes it easier to self-reflect than having a cousin come to visit. More specifically, a cousin who looks exactly like you, but acts completely differently. TV has employed the identical cousin plotline—beloved for its opportunity to give the show's stars juicy "dual roles"—since the days of Patty and her identical cousin Cathy on *The Patty Duke Show*. Foreign twins cousins with opposite personalities are also unusually common in TV land, from Steve's Scottish nobleman cousin on *My Three Sons* to Phillip Drummond's stern Dutch cousin Anna and Kimberly Drummond's mischief-making cousin Hans on *Diff'rent Strokes*. (Even *The Hughley's* Dave has an identically hillbilly cousin named DuWayne!) These paradoxical cousins are perfect for giving their counterpoints a glimpse of what could have been. What if Uncle Jesse on *Full House* had grown up in Greece? What if *The Brady Bunch*'s Alice had been an Army drill sergeant? What if Agarn on *F Troop* was a Mexican bandit? What if Samantha from *Bewitched* had dark hair? So if you're struggling with the "what-ifs" of your own life, try visiting your identical cousin. And if you don't have one, never fear: like *McHale's Navy*'s Guiseppe McHale, he could be of the "long-lost" variety.

"I never lie. I willfully engage in a campaign of misinformation."

David Duchovny as Fox Mulder on *The X- Files*

"I'm not a SNITCHER; I just tell it like it is."

Susan Olsen as Cindy Brady on *The Brady Bunch*

"I'm not sad, I'm complicated. Chicks dig that."

Hugh Laurie as Dr. Gregory House on *House*

"My first name's MISTER. My middle name's that little dot. My last name's T!"

Mr. T on *Diff'rent Strokes*

"I'm not a fascist, I'm a priest. FASCISTS dress in black and go around telling people what to do, whereas...priests...."

Dermot Morgan as Father Ted Crilly on *Father Ted*

"My name might as well be FATTY McBUTTERPANTS."

Kevin James as Doug Heffernan on *The King of Queens*

"There's nothing WORSE than a smart-ass automobile."

William Daniels as the voice of K.I.T.T. on *Knight Rider*

"They don't keep people like us in HELL, dear. We'd end up running the place."

Constance Towers as Helena Cassadine on *General Hospital*

"A CONSCIENCE is like a boat or a car. If you feel you need one, rent it."

Larry Hagman as J.R. Ewing on *Dallas*

CHAPTER 9

Making Fun of Others:

One of the Many Ways to Improve Self-Esteem

In TV land, characters deal with self-esteem issues in many ways: visiting an old friend, telling someone off, getting a makeover, getting an *extreme* makeover...but no way is more universal than teasing those around you. The art of the put-down has been highly refined over the years, even getting its own reality show on MTV in 2006. So try out some of the put-downs in the pages that follow, or make up some of your own. Because even if it doesn't make you feel better, it will definitely get a laugh.

"If you can't say anything nice, SAY IT ABOUT DIANE."

Rhea Perlman as Carla Tortelli on *Cheers*

"Suzanne, if sex were FAST FOOD, there'd be an ARCH over your bed!

Dixie Carter as Julia Sugarbaker on *Designing Women*

"I treat my body as a TEMPLE, Laverne. You have chosen to treat yours as an AMUSEMENT PARK."

Cindy Williams as Shirley Feeney on *Laverne & Shirley*

"Hey Jisela, get off the HO TRAIN...'cause you're the only one on it!"

Coral Smith on *The Real World: Back to New York*

Quiz: TV Bullies

Life is cruel, and so is TV. That's why every show needs a bully—someone to represent the forces bringing us down in our own lives, and more importantly, someone for our favorite characters to overcome.

1. Forest Whitaker, who plays Lt. Jon Kavanaugh on *The Shield*, made one of his first TV appearances as a bully on which show?

    a. *Silver Spoons*   b. *Punky Brewster*

    c. *Diff'rent Strokes*   d. *Family Ties*

2. Which is not a Springfield Elementary bully on *The Simpsons*?

    a. Rocky   b. Jimbo   c. Dolph   d. Kearny

3. On a classic episode of *The Andy Griffith Show*, Andy advises Opie to respond to a bully by taking the hit, laughing, and then

    a. running away "like a kite in the wind"

    b. standing his ground "like a totem poll in a hurricane"

    c. being gentle "like a summer breeze through the reeds"

    d. hitting back "like a windmill in a tornado"

4. The girls at school won't give Romeo any love on *The Steve Harvey Show* when a female bully known by what nickname takes an interest in him?

    a. The Bear   b. The Ox   c. The Fox   d. The Lion

Answers: 1. c 2. a 3. d 4. b

"Do you really believe in your wildest dreams that a GIRL LIKE THIS could possibly be interested in an aging, brilliantine, STICK-INSECT like yourself?"

Prunella Scales as Sybil Fawlty on *Fawlty Towers*

"If you had what other men have, I wouldn't need BATTERIES."

Katey Sagal as Peg Bundy on *Married...with Children*

"You have the morals of a RABBIT, the character of a SLUG, and the brain of a PLATYPUS."

Cybill Shepherd as Maddie Hayes on *Moonlighting*

"That man is nuttier than a SQUIRREL'S CHEEKS in October."

Rebecca Schull as Fay on *Wings*

"I suggest the FISH—has lots of bones in it, hopefully you'll choke to death."

Leslie Charleson as Dr. Monica Quartermaine on *General Hospital*

"You got a lot of MORONS in your family? 'Cause that could be genetic."

Dennis Franz as Det. Andy Sipowicz on *NYPD Blue*

"Ignatowski's got a father? Well, there goes my SPORE theory!"

Danny DeVito as Louie DePalma on *Taxi*

"You'll have to excuse my mother. She suffered a slight stroke a few years ago which rendered her TOTALLY ANNOYING."

Bea Arthur as Dortohy Zbornak on *The Golden Girls*

"I don't have low self-esteem... I have LOW ESTEEM for everyone else."

Tracy Grandstaff as the voice of Daria Morgendorffer on *Daria*

"At this point, the length of this conversation is WAY out of proportion to my interest in it."

Josh Charles as Dan Rydell on *Sports Night*

"Wait, I just REMEMBERED something! You're boring and my legs work."

David Spade as Dennis Finch on *Just Shoot Me*

Life-Changing Decisions

When you're having self-esteem issues, sometimes a little make-over will do the trick to make you feel like you've got what it takes. If you've got an itch for change, maybe cutting your hair, sprucingup that bright collared shirt, or testing out a red lipstick will serve as a quick pick-me-up. For instance, after her romantic entanglements become too much, Felicity Porter chops her long curly locks as a metaphor for letting go of her past dorm-room dramas. However, there are times when you're feeling so bad about yourself you might feel the need for major change. On *Taxi*, the lovable Latka decides to alter his image entirely, opting to become a fast lane–taking, womanizing guy's guy. But beware: a drastic life change such as this may not always last. As is often the case in television, total life makeovers typically stick for the duration of one mere episode—such as when Blanche Devereaux's father, Big Daddy, sells the family plantation to pursue a career in country music, only to realize post-performance that he has zero singing talent. So, before you go and sell Grandma's heirlooms, be sure to put some thought into your strategy for lifestyle rejuvenation— unless all it'll take is a haircut.

"Bobby, if STUPIDITY were a crime, your ass would be in jail for life!"

Steve Harris as Eugene Young on *The Practice*

"You guys are as funny as a PORK CHOP AT A BAR MITZVAH."

Melonie Haller as Angie Globogowski on *Welcome Back, Kotter*

"Off my case, TOILET FACE."

John Travolta as Vinnie Barbarino on *Welcome Back, Kotter*

"I thought about building you a boat to survive the RIVER OF TEARS I'm crying for you, but the world's smallest violins just aren't a reliable source of lumber, and that CROSS you're nailing yourself to seems buoyant enough anyways."

Hugh Laurie as Dr. Gregory House on *House*

"Your lips, my ass. THEY SHOULD MEET."

Ken Jenkins as Dr. Bob Kelso on *Scrubs*

"You know, kids, Drew's head is just like a PIÑATA. If you hit his head enough times when he's sleeping, candy comes out."

Kathy Kinney as Mimi Bobeck on *The Drew Carey Show*

"Did your brain come PREASSEMBLED, or did you glue it together yourself?"

Scott Baio as Charles on *Charles in Charge*

"I wouldn't believe you if your TONGUE came notarized!"

Judge Marilyn Milian on *The People's Court*

"I'm beginning to think ER stands for 'Everyone's Retarded.'"

Paul McCrane as Dr. Robert Romano on *ER*

"News flash Dr. Brown, you're not here to SAVE THE WORLD. Only to annoy it."

Tom Amandes as Dr. Harold Abbott Jr. on *Everwood*

"Oh, Laurie, I remembered I can't loan you the Vista Cruiser on account of I HATE YOU."

Topher Grace as Eric Forman on *That '70s Show*

"Without being rude, you're one of those packages you get at Christmastime where you say, 'CAN I GIVE IT BACK?'"

Simon Cowell on *American Idol*

"Well, someone has her RUDE HAT on tonight."

Alfonso Ribeiro as Carlton Banks on *The Fresh Prince of Bel-Air*

Quiz: Famous TV Guest Stars

Nothing lifts your self-worth (and the ratings) like knowing that someone famous will take a little time out of his or her busy schedule to drop by. Can you answer the following questions, all about famous TV guest stars?

1. In a 1966 episode of *Gunsmoke*, which legend of the silver screen guest stars as Ma Stone, an angry rancher out for revenge after the hanging of her husband?

2. This groovy '70s teen gets herself into a bit of a pickle when she promises her peers a prom-night appearance by Davy Jones. As luck would have it, the teen idol saves the day.

3. When Archie Bunker takes a job driving a taxi, which superstar crooner makes one of the greatest guest appearances in TV history when he leaves his briefcase in Archie's cab?

4. This White House matriarch touts the importance of drug prevention to the Jackson-Drummonds on a special episode of *Diff'rent Strokes*.

5. When this silent star visits *I Love Lucy*, he and Lucy enact a "mirror scene" in which they match comic wits as they mimic each other's every move.

6. Pop-art celebrity Andy Warhol was on board for an episode of this romantic Aaron Spelling hit.

Answers: 1. Bette Davis 2. Marsha Brady 3. Sammy Davis Jr. 4. Nancy Reagan 5. Harpo Marx 6. *The Love Boat*

"My dad always told me that if you have nothing nice to say, you shouldn't say anything at all. Well, my daddy's not here, and you're a WEENIE!"

Mary-Kate or Ashley Olsen as Michelle Tanner on *Full House*

"Lady, don't take this the wrong way, but you're NUTS!"

Jon Lovitz as the voice of Jay Sherman on *The Critic*

"You know I'm not about to go to Texas and not ride the mechanical bull, Chelina. That would be like going to Los Angeles and not sleeping with PARIS HILTON."

James Spader as Alan Shore on *Boston Legal*

"These guns are identical to the one that killed Jim Johnson. Watch carefully as I test fire this gun into these videotapes of BARBARA WALTERS INTERVIEWS."

Ed Williams as Ted Olson on *Police Squad!*

"Whoa! Where you going in those pants, 1982?"

Courteney Cox Arquette as Monica Geller on *Friends*

"You know your eyebrows GOT MARRIED, right?"

Mo'Nique as Nikki Parker on *The Parkers*

"Klinger, you are a GENTLEMAN and a LADY."

David Ogden Stiers as
Maj. Charles Emerson Winchester III on *M*A*S*H*

"I'm not interested. If the world was destroyed and you were the LAST MAN within a thousand mile radius, I would SWIM ACROSS THE OCEAN on a rumor that Screech from *Saved by the Bell* was spotted in Japan."

Ellen DeGeneres as Ellen Morgan on *Ellen*

"I didn't say EVERY GUY was a jerk. I said YOU were a jerk."

Tangi Miller as Elena Tyler on *Felicity*

"Ooo, she's so COLD, sweetie! I'll just bet she has her period in cubes."

Jennifer Saunders as Eddy Monsoon on *Absolutely Fabulous*

"May the WINDS OF THE SAHARA blow a scorpion up your sister's caftan."

Johnny Carson as Carnac the Magnificent on *The Tonight Show*

"I'm the captain of the ship of fools."

Gavin MacLeod as Capt. Merrill Stubing on *The Love Boat*

CHAPTER 10

Setting Goals

and Movin' On Up

If you're ever going to finally get a piece of that pie, you'll first have to set some goals. So resolve to lose some weight, conquer your fears, or watch an entire season of *24* in one sitting. Whatever your goal, you'll have TV to help you achieve it by showing you examples of characters who have kicked drugs, outwitted motorcycle gangs, and even uncovered vast alien conspiracies—when they put their minds to it. With a little mind power and a dab of elbow grease, you too can make a difference in your own life.

"Sometimes it's the SMALLEST DECISIONS that can change your life forever."

Keri Russell as Felicity Porter on *Felicity*

"I tried to get Al to fix the driveway a long time ago. But his philosophy is why improve a home you're only going to LIVE IN anyway?"

Katey Sagal as Peg Bundy on *Married...with Children*

"You put a LIVING ROOM where the CRACK DEN used to be!"

Carson Kressley on *Queer Eye for the Straight Guy*

"The difficult thing about being a MASS MURDERER isn't the murdering part. It's the mass part. By around the seventh murder you're likely to feel like you're IN A RUT. It's like what happened the other day: I had just finished ending a human life in a SENSELESS ACT OF VIOLENCE when I run into this old friend of mine from high school. And he says, 'Hey! Whatcha been doin'?' And I think to myself, 'What HAVE I been doing? Where's this leading? Am I gonna be doing this at FIFTY?' Sometimes I think I really should GO BACK TO COLLEGE."

Dave Foley as a mass murderer on *Kids in the Hall*

"I have one son who's about to become my DAUGHTER, another son whom people are trying to KILL, I have a LUNATIC STEPSON AND A DUMMY living in my home."

Cathryn Damon as Mary Campbell on *Soap*

"You know, Dick, when life gives you lemons, just shut up and EAT THE DAMN LEMONS."

French Stewart as Harry Solomon on *3rd Rock from the Sun*

Life Lesson

Fear Not!

There's no need to let your fears keep you from a fulfilling life. Grab hold of those needless anxieties and take steps to conquer them. If possible, try to confront your fear head-on, like attorney Alan Shore of *Boston Legal*, whose crippling fear of clowns impedes his ability to question a defendant: Zozo the Clown. Only when he exposes himself to his lifelong neurosis—by squeezing Zozo's big, red nose—is Shore cured for good. This technique also works for *Bonanza*'s Little Joe Cartwright, who is so terrified of heights that his nightmares keep Pa and his brothers up every night—until Pa decides to make him face his acrophobia head-on. If facing your fears isn't enough, you may need professional help. Therapy sessions help Marge Simpson uncover the deep-seated trauma that brought about her fear of flying: the childhood discovery that her father was employed as an airplane steward. Luckily, in this day and age we have the wise and mighty Dr. Phil, who advises that "walking through your fears" is the most successful strategy in beating them. So, armed with your most comfortable walking shoes, take that first step to complete autonomy without looking back.

"I PITY THE FOOL who goes out tryin' to take over the world, then runs home cryin' to his momma!"

Mr. T as Bosco "B.A." Baracus on *The A-Team*

"I am trying so hard to feel sorry for you, but you're just SO PATHETIC that it's making me double over with cruel, internal silent laughter."

Leslie Grossman as Mary Cherry on *Popular*

"I'LL QUIT COFFEE. It won't be easy drinking my BAILEY'S STRAIGHT, but I'll get used to it. It'll still be the best part of waking up."

Megan Mullally as Karen Walker on *Will & Grace*

"I swear with God as my witness, I will NEVER pick up another man!...in a library...on a Saturday... unless he's cute...and drives a nice car....Amen."

Rue McClanahan as Blanche Devereaux on *The Golden Girls*

"Put your clothes on, get out of here, and CHANGE YOUR TASTE IN MEN."

Michael Chiklis as Det. Vic Mackey on *The Shield*

"I wanna do it, Gus. I wanna see that country, before the BANKERS and LAWYERS all git it."

Tommy Lee Jones as Woodrow Call on *Lonesome Dove*

"Why don't I put a STAKE through her heart. You'd be surprised at how many things that'll kill."

Sarah Michelle Gellar as Buffy Summers on *Buffy the Vampire Slayer*

"I don't have that much experience saying NO to women. I mean, the closest I've ever gotten is, 'Not now, we're landing.'"

Ted Danson as Sam Malone on *Cheers*

"I'm not AGAINST half-naked girls...well, not as often as I'd like to be."

Benny Hill on *The Benny Hill Show*

"The subject was booked under SECTION 01—in danger of leading an idle, dissolute, or immoral life."

Jack Webb as Sgt. Joe Friday on *Dragnet*

Quiz: TV Ratings

There's no goal loftier for a TV show than high ratings. And just as each show aspires to be the best, so should you! Can you answer these questions about television ratings?

1. Which of the following classic sitcoms held the longest streak as television's most-watched program?
   a. *Seinfeld*   b. *Cheers*   c. *I Love Lucy*   d. *All in the Family*

2. Which of the dueling primetime dramas *Dallas* and *Dynasty* spent more time at the top of the ratings chart?

3. True or false: *Survivor: Australian Outback* was the first reality show to woo enough TV viewers to score the number one ratings spot of the year.

4. What novel-turned-miniseries garnered an audience of 38.8 million, making it the most-watched miniseries in the history of television and the third-most-watched TV event ever?

5. Which of the following TV Westerns had the best track record with viewers?
   a. *Bonanza*   b. *Gunsmoke*   c. *The Lone Ranger*   d. *Maverick*

6. True or false: The series finale of *M*A*S*H* had the most viewers of any TV show in history, with more than 50 million households tuning in.

Answers: 1. d 2. *Dallas* 3. true 4. *Roots* 5. b 6. true

"The SECRET TO SUCCESS, whether it's women or money, is knowing WHEN TO QUIT. I oughta know: I'm divorced and broke.

Don Johnson as Det. James "Sonny" Crockett on *Miami Vice*

"Never argue with an IDIOT. They drag you down to their level and then beat you with experience."

Daniel Stern as the voice of Dilbert on *Dilbert*

"Gee, Dad, I have enough trouble keeping MYSELF good without keeping all the other kids good."

Jerry Mathers as Beaver Cleaver on *Leave It to Beaver*

"I've found from past experiences: the tighter your plan the more likely you are to run into something UNPREDICTABLE."

Richard Dean Anderson as Angus MacGyver on *MacGyver*

"Sometimes you just have to let the UNIVERSE tell you what to do."

Jenna Elfman as Dharma on *Dharma & Greg*

"Mom, I need to REEVALUATE MY LIFE. Do you have a minute?"

Justine Bateman as Mallory Keaton on *Family Ties*

"College is for UGLY GIRLS who can't get modeling contracts."

Ashton Kutcher as Michael Kelso on *That '70s Show*

"College is for women who don't wanna MARRY THE FIRST IDIOT THEY MEET and squeeze out his bastard, moron children."

Laura Prepon as Donna Pinciotti on *That '70s Show*

"Sometimes, LETTING GO is the only way to move forward."

Tom Welling as Clark Kent on *Smallville*

"I was lying in bed last night and I couldn't sleep, and I came up with an idea. So I went RIGHT HOME and wrote it down."

Betty White as Sue Ann Nivens on *The Mary Tyler Moore Show*

"If you want to receive e-mails about my upcoming shows, please GIVE ME MONEY so I can buy a computer."

Lisa Kudrow as Phoebe Buffay on *Friends*

The Battle of the Bulge

One of the most common goals people set for themselves is taking off those extra pounds. But the desire to lose weight can drive us to take some drastic actions. For example, when Uncle Fester Addams vows to lose weight before his French pen-pal arrives for their first encounter, he exercises feverishly to TV aerobics, hypnotizes himself, and uses a mummy case (what else?) as a steam bath to sweat off his pounds. When Lucy Ricardo is promised a slot as a dancer in Ricky's show—if she can lose twelve pounds in four days—she starves herself, exercises, and locks herself in a steam cabinet until she can squeeze her way into the act...and then proceeds to faint from exhaustion and undernourishment. If you're not up for a sauna and are considering a diet instead, be sure not to let food consume your every waking thought. Take a tip from Cliff Huxtable, whose food problems result in a twisted nightmare involving a tornado that whisks Claire out the window, a stint in the Navy under the command of Theo (who chastises Cliff for his poor eating habits), and Muppet surgeons operating on him. Clearly, it's easy to get carried away with weight-loss fever, so refrain from jumping on the fad-diet wagon and make healthy eating part of your daily regimen.

"It's just like the story of the GRASSHOPPER and the OCTOPUS. All year long, the grasshopper kept BURYING ACORNS for the winter, while the octopus MOOCHED off his girlfriend and watched TV. But then the winter came, and the grasshopper died, and the octopus ate all his acorns. And also he GOT A RACECAR. Is any of this getting through to you?"

Billy West as the voice of Fry on *Futurama*

"You know, my father smoked a lot...he's been smoking for YEARS. He tried to quit, he tried everything, you know. He tried hypnosis, and it didn't really take, and then he tried THAT THING with all the needles, what do they call that... heroin...."

Bill Braudis as the voice of Bill on *Dr. Katz, Professional Therapist*

"I didn't know you're only supposed to wear one NICOTINE PATCH at a time."

Phil Hartman as Bill McNeal on *NewsRadio*

"Sometimes we get SO ATTACHED to things that it becomes hard to move on. Things like old cars... bad relationships...my pet snake who loved to sleep in the driveway...."

Dan Milano as the voice of Greg on *Greg the Bunny*

"We were THROWN TOGETHER against our will, and we're all just trying to make the best of it until we can get the chance to SCREW THE OTHERS to get what we want."

Jonathan Hardy as the voice of Dominar Rygel XVI on *Farscape*

"A man's gotta do what a man's gotta do. AND SO DO I."

Dick Van Dyke as Rob Petrie on *The Dick van Dyke Show*

"The BEST REWARDS come when you risk the most. Sometimes, the risk is its own reward."

Neil Patrick Harris as Doogie Howser on *Doogie Howser, M.D.*

CHAPTER 11

Some Questions Can Never Be Answered

(Even on *Jeopardy!*)

What is the meaning of life? Is there a God? Will the public ever get sick of *American Idol*? If these types of questions keep you up at night, TV is a great place to turn. Not because it can answer any of these elusive queries, but because it will take your mind off the more challenging aspects of life. Ponder the easier questions from TV game shows, or watch people make fools of themselves on sitcoms or reality shows. And if your mind is still aching, there's always one last way to extinguish all thought: infomercials.

"If we had to pick an island to get marooned on, why didn't we pick MANHATTAN?"

Tina Louise as Ginger Grant on *Gilligan's Island*

"How come whenever my SHIP COMES IN, it's leaking?"

Bea Arthur as Dorothy Zbornak on *The Golden Girls*

"CONVICTIONS AND BELIEFS. What do they have to do with religion?"

Tim Allen as Tim Taylor on *Home Improvement*

$Quiz$: Game Shows

If only we could use a lifeline when it comes to the bigger questions in life. Can you match the catchphrase on the left with the game show on the right that made it famous?

1. Survey says...

2. No whammys!

3. I'd like to buy a vowel.

4. We'll take the physical challenge.

5. Come on down!

6. Is it bigger than a bread box?

7. Pick your briefcase.

8. It's a daily double!

9. Let's see what's behind door number one!

10. Is that your final answer?

a. *The Price Is Right*

b. *Deal or No Deal*

c. *Let's Make a Deal*

d. *Jeopardy!*

e. *Double Dare*

f. *Family Feud*

g. *Who Wants to Be a Millionaire?*

h. *Wheel of Fortune*

i. *Press Your Luck*

j. *What's My Line?*

Answers: 1. f 2. i 3. h 4. e 5. a 6. j 7. b 8. d 9. c 10. g

"How would you like to sit through two people in their sixties fighting over WHO INVENTED THE LAWN?"

Patricia Heaton as Debra Barone on *Everybody Loves Raymond*

"You know, we're not the ONLY ONES destroying trees. What about beavers? You call yourself an environmentalist, why don't you go club a few beavers?"

Portia de Rossi as Lindsay Funke on *Arrested Development*

"I know YOU are but what am I?"

Paul Reubens as Pee-Wee Herman on *Pee-Wee's Playhouse*

"Who would win in a fight: a BIG STRONG GUY or an INVISIBLE FAT GUY?"

Josh Randall as Dr. Mike Burton on *Ed*

"What's the WORST that can happen? So the tornado picks up our house and slams it down in a better neighborhood."

Roseanne as Roseanne Conner on *Roseanne*

"How come we OVERCAME and nobody told me?"

Marla Gibbs as Florence Johnston on *The Jeffersons*

"What is WAL-MART? Do they, like, sell wall stuff?"

Paris Hilton on *The Simple Life*

"IS THIS CHICKEN OR IS THIS FISH? I know it's tuna. But it says chicken by the sea."

Jessica Simpson on *Newlyweds*

"Where would we be without the agitators of the world attaching the ELECTRODES OF KNOWLEDGE to the nipples of ignorance?"

John Lithgow as Dr. Dick Solomon on *3rd Rock from the Sun*

"What is the different type of hash out there? We all know that it's called the bionic, the BOMB, the puff, the blow, the black, the HERB, the sensie, the chronic, the SWEET MARY JANE, the shit, Ganja, split, reefer, the bad, the Buddha, the HOME GROWN, the ill, the Maui, the method, pot, lethal turbo, Thai, SHAKE, SKUNK, STRESS, whacky, weed, glaze, the boot, dime bag, SCOOBY DOO, Bob, bogey, backyard BOOGIE. But what is the other terms for it?"

Sacha Baron Cohen as Ali G on *The Ali G Show*

"Do you know how hard it is to get a nicotine patch to STICK TO A MONKEY?"

Shae D'Lyn as Jane Cavanaugh on *Dharma & Greg*

"TALK AMONGST YOURSELVES. I'll give you a topic. A peanut: it's neither a pea nor a nut, discuss."

Mike Meyers as Linda Richman on *Saturday Night Live*

"One morning I shot a LION in my pajamas. Now, what he was doing in my PAJAMAS, I'll never know!"

Paul Lind as Uncle Arthur on *Bewitched*

• Life Lesson •

Seeing the Light

When you've been pondering the deep questions of this world, nothing helps you see the true meaning of life like a near-death experience. Whether it's an electrocution like Schneider's on *One Life to Live*, the largest bee sting ever like Leela's on *Futurama*, or run-of-the mill heart surgery like Niles's on *Fraiser*, being close to death makes you enjoy the little things in life. Getting a glimpse of the other side can also help you realize who is important to you. On *Family Guy*, after Peter is struck by lightning he realizes he needs to pay more attention to his wife, Lois (and gives the Grim Reaper a couple of dating tips). Be aware, however, that those around you may not share your new lease on life. After Ted Baxter tries to get his loved ones to see the beauty in a grain of salt one too many times on *The Mary Tyler Moore Show*, they're ready to bring him close to death again. And on *3rd Rock from the Sun*, Dick is so jealous of Sally, Harry, and Tommy's new insights after a chandelier almost crushes them that he tries putting himself in the way of danger so he can have a near-death experience of his own. So although watching it on TV can be helpful, perhaps being close to death falls into the category of "don't try this at home."

"How can we POSSIBLY use sex to get what we want? Sex IS what we want."

Kelsey Grammer as Frasier Crane on *Frasier*

"You know what blows my mind? Women can see breasts ANY TIME they want. You just look down, and there they are. How you get ANY work done is beyond me."

Matt LeBlanc as Joey Tribbiani on *Friends*

"If Hugh Hefner truly thinks that being publicly spread-eagled is so FANTASTIC, how come we haven't seen his little WAHOO with a staple in the middle?"

Dixie Carter as Julia Sugarbaker on *Designing Women*

"How do you ACCIDENTALLY kiss someone? Did she slip on a rug, and your lips broke her fall?"

Danielle Fishel as Topanga Lawrence on *Boy Meets World*

"I was just decorating my Christmas tree and I was wondering, is there a TRICK to stringing cranberry sauce?"

Bill Daily as Howard Borden on *The Bob Newhart Show*

"How can I have so much BAD LUCK with four horseshoes?"

Allan Lane as the voice of Mister Ed on *Mister Ed*

"If Abraham Lincoln thought that being president was a LONG SHOT and gave up, we would have nobody's picture on the five dollar bill."

Henry Winkler as Arthur "the Fonz" Fonzarelli on *Happy Days*

Quiz: Science Fiction

Some of TV's most unanswerable questions have come from science-fiction shows. Can you answer the questions below, hopefully none of which pertain to your own life?

1. True or false: On *The X-Files*, Mulder and Scully discover that if you are vaccinated against chicken pox you can't be infected by "the black oil."

2. In the 1963 classic episode of *The Twilight Zone* "Nightmare at 20,000 Feet," a young William Shatner stars as the only man who can see what?

3. On *Lost*, the castaways of the mystical island keep running into which series of numbers?
   a. 7, 8, 19, 13, 43, 22   b. 4, 8, 15, 16, 23, 42
   c. 7, 8, 27, 33, 48, 52   d. 6, 8, 36, 37, 44, 42

4. *Saturday Night Live*'s most popular aliens, the Coneheads, claimed to be from what country?

5. True or false: The original *Star Trek* was the shortest-running series in the *Star Trek* franchise.

6. To protest the cancellation of the hit show *Roswell*, fans sent thousands of bottles of what to network execs?

Answers: 1. false 2. a creature on the wing of the plane 3. b 4. France 5. true 6. Tabasco sauce

"If you ever reach total enlightenment while drinking beer, I bet it makes beer shoot out your nose."

Jack Handey on *Saturday Night Live*

"Do you think when they order AMERICAN take-out
in China they have trouble using FORKS?"

Kim Coles as Synclaire James on *Living Single*

"What the hell kind of country is this if I can only
hate a man if he's white?"

Mike Judge as Hank Hill on *King of the Hill*

"How do you spell 'S'PERIENCE?'"

Desi Arnaz as Ricky Ricardo on *I Love Lucy*

"GRASSHOPPER, a man may tell himself many things. But is a man's universe made only of himself?"

Keye Luke as Master Po on *Kung Fu*

"Do BEARS bear? Do BEES be?

Bruce Willis as David Addison on *Moonlighting*

"You are about FIVE DIFFERENT KINDS of crazy, you know that?"

Peter Krause as Casey McCall on *Sports Night*

"Sometimes the only SANE answer to an INSANE world is INSANITY."

David Duchovny as Fox Mulder on *The X-Files*

CHAPTER 12

final
Advice

and Other
Non Sequiturs

If you've come this far then you've learned a lot. But before you change the channel, don't forget about TV's most powerful medium: the one-liner. A good one-liner can come from anywhere—a friend, a grandparent, a video store clerk, even a stranger on the street—and can be identified by its usage in commercials for the show or "next time on..." segments. Keep your ears open for these little gems of wisdom, both in front of the TV and in your own life. Because you never know where your next piece of great advice is going to come from.

"You know what they say: you can lead a herring to water, but you have to walk REALLY FAST or he'll die."

Betty White as Rose Nylund on *The Golden Girls*

"Diane, never drink coffee that has been ANYWHERE NEAR a fish."

Kyle MacLachlan as Special Agent Dale Cooper on *Twin Peaks*

"Due to the shape of the North American elk's esophagus, even if it could speak, it could not pronounce the word LASAGNA."

John Ratzenberger as Cliff Clavin on *Cheers*

"A PAPERCLIP can be a wondrous thing. More times than I can remember, one of these has gotten me out of a tight spot."

Richard Dean Anderson as Angus MacGyver on *MacGyver*

"The commandment says, 'Thou shalt not kill.' It does not say, 'Thou shalt not kill ONLY NICE PEOPLE.'"

Michael Moriarty as Ben Stone on *Law & Order*

"'NICE' is goodbye at the door."

Susan Saint James as Kate McArdle on *Kate & Allie*

"A SONG and a SNACK can turn any moment into an occasion."

Peter Paige as Emmett Honeycutt on *Queer as Folk*

"You know, my friends, it's better to LOOK good than to FEEL good...you know what I'm telling you."

Billy Crystal as Fernando Lamas on *Saturday Night Live*

"Always keep your bowler on in time of stress, and watch out for DIABOLICAL MASTERMINDS."

Diana Rigg as Emma Peel on *The Avengers*

Quiz: The Final Episode

Nothing is more important than the final episode of a television show, where viewers get one last chance to learn something from the characters they've grown to love. For each show below, choose what happened on its final episode.

1. *Cheers*
   a. Diane receives an award for writing a cable miniseries
   b. Sam receives an award for sports writing
   c. Cliff receives an award at a trivia contest

2. *The Mary Tyler Moore Show*
   a. Ted gets fired   b. everyone but Ted gets fired   c. Mary gets engaged

3. *Seinfeld*
   a. Jerry and Elaine get back together
   b. Jerry decides to move to LA
   c. Jerry, George, Elaine, and Kramer end up in jail

4. *M*A*S*H*
   a. Klinger is finally found to be mentally unfit for duty
   b. Klinger decides to stay in Korea with his new wife
   c. Klinger starts a fire that burns down the camp

Answers: 1. b 2. b 3. c 4. b

"I hope if dogs ever TAKE OVER THE WORLD, and they chose a king, they don't just go by size, because I bet there are some Chihuahuas with some good ideas."

Jack Handey on *Saturday Night Live*

"Help control the pet population. HAVE YOUR PET SPAYED OR NEUTERED."

Bob Barker on *The Price Is Right*

"Just because you're PARANOID, it doesn't mean they're not out to get you."

David Duchovny as Fox Mulder on *The X-Files*

"Barnes just broke the cardinal rule in politics: never get caught in bed with a DEAD WOMAN or a LIVE MAN."

Larry Hagman as J.R. Ewing on *Dallas*

"Real men don't use instructions, son. Besides, this is just the MANUFACTURER'S OPINION of how to put this together."

Tim Allen as Tim Taylor on *Home Improvement*

"If Moses had been a woman, leading the Jews out of Egypt, she'd have stopped to ask for directions. They would've found Israel within a WEEK."

Mary Page Keller as Grace Bridges on *Commander in Chief*

"Civilization will not advance ONE IOTA until they start putting more toilets in the ladies' room."

Harriet Samson Harris as Bebe Glazer on *Frasier*

"I just don't trust ANYTHING that bleeds for five days and doesn't die."

Trey Parker as the voice of Mr. Garrison on *South Park*

"Like wars, most fights are started by people who WON'T GET HIT."

Chris Rock as narrator Chris on *Everybody Hates Chris*

"When a man carries a gun all the time, the RESPECT he thinks he's getting might really be FEAR."

Andy Griffith as Andy Taylor on *The Andy Griffith Show*

"They say 'GUNS don't kill people, people kill people.' But that's like saying, 'Butter knives don't spread butter on bread, people spread butter on bread.' Of course, that's true, but that doesn't make it a SMART THING to say."

Ian Gomez as Javier Frantata on *Felicity*

"A man's never WRONG doing what he thinks is right."

Lorne Greene as Ben Cartwright on *Bonanza*

"Sometimes, the hardest thing to do is to do NOTHING."

William Peterson as Gil Grissom on *CSI: Crime Scene Investigation*

"A WISE MAN is nothing but a fool with a good memory."

Gerald McRaney as Russell Greene on *Promised Land*

"Dumb people are always BLISSFULLY UNAWARE of how dumb they are."

Bill Fagerbakke as the voice of Patrick Star
on *Spongebob Squarepants*

• Life Lesson •

Under the Influence

If you're not sure where to get advice, one thing's for certain: don't listen to motivational speakers. Perhaps best exemplified by the greasy and overbearing Matt Foley of *Saturday Night Live* (who lives in a van down by the river and isn't afraid to tell you so), these professional advice-givers have appeared on everything from *8 Simple Rules* to *Ellen* to *Beavis and Butt-head*. Although some motivational speakers are just unsuccessful at getting their listeners to attain their goals—like the speaker who fails to help a monster stop eating human brains on *The X-Files*—some give advice that goes completely awry, such as when Drew Carey takes some advice from a seminar and ends up with a bull and a camel running rampant through his office's boardroom. Then there are those who are downright evil, like the former motivational speaker who runs a cult of vampires on *Angel*, and the motivational speaker who persuades his followers to kill on *Law & Order: CI*. And if you need any further proof that motivational speakers are bad luck, take the case of Bob Patterson, the speaker brought to life by Jason Alexander on his own show in 2001: the series lasted only five episodes.

"There's an old Polish proverb that says 'ONLY THE CENTIPEDE can hear all the footsteps of his uncle.'"

George Peppard as Thomas Banacek on *Banacek*

"It's just like my Aunt Agnes used to say, 'You might have the WHOLE WORLD at your feet, but that don't stop the corns from hurtin'.'"

Rose Marie as Sally Rogers on *The Dick Van Dyke Show*

"Yes, each new day in suburbia brings with it a new set of lies. The worst are the ones we tell ourselves right before we fall asleep. We whisper them in the dark, telling ourselves we're HAPPY, or that he's happy. That we can CHANGE, or that he will change his mind. We persuade ourselves that we can LIVE WITH OUR SINS, or that we can live without him. Yes, each night before we fall asleep we lie to ourselves in a desperate, desperate hope that come morning IT WILL ALL BE TRUE."

Brenda Strong as Mary Alice Young on *Desperate Housewives*

"The more things change, the more they STAY THE SAME. I'm not sure who the first person was who said that. Probably Shakespeare. Or maybe Sting."

Gregory Smith as Ephram Brown on *Everwood*

"I've experienced life, and I'm here to tell you it's OVERRATED."

Candice Bergen as Murphy Brown on *Murphy Brown*

"BAD NEWS comes in all packages."

Kathryn Erbe as Det. Alexandra Eames on *Law & Order: CI*

"An OPTIMIST says, 'The drink is half full.' A PESSIMIST says, 'The drink is half full, but I might have bowel cancer.'"

Bruce McCulloch as Mr. B. on *Kids in the Hall*

"Sometimes the road less traveled is LESS TRAVELED for a reason."

Jerry Seinfeld on *Seinfeld*

"My mom said it's okay to talk to lesbians because they take good care of their cats and have a CAN-DO attitude."

Michael McDonald as Stuart Larkin on *Mad TV*

"Ain't no use running, fool! I know where your mama parks your house!"

Jason Lee as Earl on *My Name Is Earl*

"Live FAST, love HARD, and don't let anybody else use your COMB."

Henry Winkler as Arthur "the Fonz" Fonzarelli on *Happy Days*

Quiz: Theme Song Advice

The song a television show opens and closes with has the challenging task of encapsulating the show's theme in a few (often rhyming) stanzas. It also often offers a key piece of advice. Which show's theme song contains the advice listed below?

1. Now, the world don't move / to the beat of just one drum / What might be right for you / may not be right for some

2. I can't do this all on my own / No, I know I'm no Superman

3. Making your way in the world today / takes everything you've got

4. Fish don't fry in the kitchen / Beans don't burn on the grill

5. We're gonna make our dreams come true / Doin' it our way

6. In my opinionation, the sun is gonna surely shine

7. Life goes on / and so do we / just how we do it is no mystery

8. But you're one in a million / you've got that shotgun shine / Born under a bad sign, with a blue moon in your eyes

9. But it's time you started living / It's time you let someone else do some giving

10. Hustlers grab your guns / Your shadow weighs a ton / Driving down the 101

Answers: 1. *Diff'rent Strokes* 2. *Scrubs* 3. *Cheers* 4. *The Jeffersons* 5. *Laverne & Shirley* 6. *Blossom* 7. *Empty Nest* 8. *The Mary Tyler Moore Show* 9. *The Sopranos* 10. *The OC*

"Someone once said that dealing with Reptilians is like bargaining with the sun. You make NO PROGRESS, and you come away burned."

Rick Worthy as Jannar on *Star Trek: Enterprise*

"Never take a 'NO' from somebody who isn't in a position to give you a 'YES' in the first place."

Oprah Winfrey on *Oprah*

"When lift plus thrust is greater than load plus drag, any object can fly."

Sally Field as Sister Bertrille on *The Flying Nun*

"MICKEY MOUSE ain't got no race. He represents all men."

Carroll O'Connor as Archie Bunker on *All in the Family*

"The last time I saw a COWBOY with that many TATTOOS I was at a Cher concert!"

Bronson Pinchot on *The Surreal Life*

"Till next time, TAKE CARE OF YOURSELF, and each other."

Jerry Springer on *The Jerry Springer Show*

"The truth is like GRITS: you can't serve it up plain, you got to put a little salt on it."

Walton Goggins as Shane Vendrell on *The Shield*

"There are two things in the world you never want people to see how you make them—LAWS and SAUSAGES."

John Spencer as Leo McGarry on *The West Wing*

"It's better that TEN guilty men go free, than ONE innocent man suffer."

Dylan McDermott as Bobby Donnell on *The Practice*

"CHAMPAGNE wishes and CAVIAR dreams."

Robin Leach on *Lifestyles of the Rich and Famous*

"May your LIQUOR be cold, your WOMEN be hot, and may all of your PROBLEMS just slide off like snot."

Damon Wayans as Anton Jackson on *In Living Color*

"As we say in the SEWER, here's mud in your eye."

Art Carney as Ed Norton on *The Honeymooners*

INDEX

Page numbers in *italics* refer to sidebars.

B

M

"It'll turn out all right in THE END. If it's not all right, it's not THE END."

Tyne Daly as Maxine Gray on *Judging Amy*